STOCK CAR RACING

JEFF GORDON

THE NASCAR SUPERSTAR'S STORY

GLEN GRISSOM
AND THE EDITORS OF
STOCK CAR RACING MAGAZINE

MOTORBOOKS
INTERNATIONAL

First published in 2005 by Motorbooks International, an imprint of MBI Publishing Company, Galtier Plaza, Suite 200, 380 Jackson Street, St. Paul, MN 55101-3885 USA

Motorbooks International titles are also available at discounts in bulk quantity for industrial or sales-promotional use. For details write to Special Sales Manager at Motorbooks International Wholesalers & Distributors, Galtier Plaza, Suite 200, 380 Jackson Street, St. Paul, MN 55101-3885 USA.

ISBN 0-7603-2178-7

Editors: Glen Grissom and Leah Noel
Designer: Kari Johnston

Printed in China

On the cover: Jeff Gordon truly represents a new breed of racer, one groomed from childhood to become not only a successful driver on the track, but one who knows how to deal with being in the spotlight as a superstar and marketer. *Autostock*

On the frontispiece: Gordon made his first Cup appearance in the last race of 1992 at Atlanta, the same race in which legend Richard Petty ended his 30-plus year career. *Harold Hinson*

On the title page: Jeff Gordon knows how to lead laps, particularly the last one. In his 12-year career on the Cup circuit, he's already racked up 69 wins. *Nigel Kinrade*

On the back cover: Gordon chasing down Rusty Wallace in the No. 2 Miller Lite car. Wallace will retire at the end of the 2005 racing season. *Nigel Kinrade*

CONTENTS

INTRODUCTION

Jeff Gordon Races Toward the American Dream

BY GLEN GRISSOM

Some fans love Jeff Gordon, others hate him. It all really comes down to the fact that he's found unprecedented success at such a young age.
SCR Archives

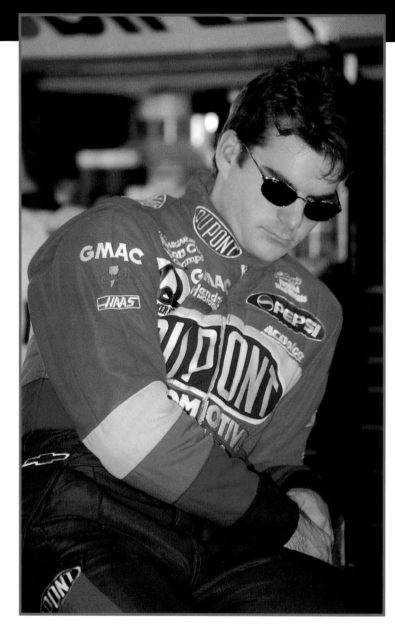

Many motorsports observers thought that when Jeff Gordon jumped from the open wheel ranks to the stock car world in the early 1990s, racing would never be the same. But most couldn't realize just how much things would change because of this young, good-looking driver who was fearless on the track and a marketing dream off it.

Now more than a decade and 69 (and counting) Cup wins later, everyone realizes Gordon's shattering impact. He ushered in a new generation of drivers when he signed with powerhouse Hendrick Motorsports in 1992, a generation in which budding talent is almost instantaneously rewarded with a top ride.

Of course, Gordon's entrance would mean little if he hadn't been so successful. After only three years in Cup racing, he became the youngest driver to win a championship in 1995, and then nearly won four championships in a row. Even though he's been just shy of earning a fifth crown in the last three years, he's the only racer in sight of meeting or exceeding the seven-championship totals of the legendary Richard Petty and Dale Earnhardt. Of course the question remains, will Jeff Gordon stay behind the wheel long enough to go for eight? No one knows, but no one questions his drive to be the best.

Gordon grew up wanting to be like Rick Mears and win the Indy 500, but instead he became Jeff Gordon, winning the first Brickyard 400 at the fabled track. He was on a well-worn path to racing open wheel Indy-type cars, but the forces that have ripped that sport asunder today were just ripening then—he couldn't bring any big bags of cash, couldn't get a ride. So he made tentative steps to the "taxi cabs" (as old-time Indy drivers derided stock cars) and the eventual attention of Rick Hendrick.

It's all too easy to forget what a magnificent gamble Gordon (and crew chief Ray Evernham) represented when Hendrick signed the Wonder Boy to a top-class car. He was no major flash in Busch racing. Ford's racing heads didn't even have him under a signed contract for a Cup ride—that's how much in regard they held him. Yet, Hendrick, in classic card shark fashion, signed Gordon faster than Ford realized he was off the table.

With 20/20 hindsight, we can see how well Hendrick's gamble paid off and exactly how much Gordon has mightily altered the racing balance in the United States. Without Jeff Gordon, there would be no Ryan Newman, Tony Stewart, Kasey Kahne, Carl Edwards, Jimmie Johnson, or Reed Sorenson, the up-and-coming stars who have even further boosted NASCAR's rising popularity. There would also be no dads in Kansas dreaming about a future stock car career for their five-year-olds, no racers being signed to development contracts at 16 for a Cup team, no racers punching out of BGN racing to Cup in only two seasons , no incredible R&D budgets and engineering staffs supporting these young wheelmen. Because of this racing and marketing phenom, the entire racing sphere has spun off its old axis, and kids don't think about growing up to be Rick Mears anymore. They want to be Jeff Gordon. This book tells you why.

Gordon tries to spend as much time as possible greeting fans, but quite frankly, because of sponsorship and media demands, he can't spend hours with the crowds the way Richard Petty did. *SCR Archives*

JEFF GORDON, WINSTON CUP SUPERSTAR?

Just How Big Will This Guy Be? Real Big!

STAFF REPORT
Stock Car Racing, February 1993

Gordon won his first big league stock car race, a Busch event at Atlanta, in March 1992. *SCR Archives*

Within a few seconds, Richard Petty, the most successful and popular big-league stock car driver of all time, strapped into his car for the final time and Jeff Gordon, the most highly rated and perhaps most talented young stock car driver since Petty's career began, strapped into a Winston Cup car for the first time. It was at once ironic and most interesting that as Petty's Winston Cup career ended, Gordon's began.

Gordon brings with him all of Tim Richmond's talent and none of the baggage. Comparisons are natural here, since both men came out of open-wheel racing: midgets, supermodifieds, sprint cars, dirt cars. Even Rich Hendrick, who fielded cars for both, sees parallels. The personalities of the two men are as far apart as Daytona and Monaco. Gordon is quiet, to himself. Richmond was wild-eyed and outgoing. Gordon is completely focused on racing. Richmond was distracted by women, glamour, Hollywood, and even boats. It's only the ability to win and a heritage of open-wheel racing that is similar.

Predicting great success for this kid is a no-brainer because Gordon has already delivered so much. In 1992, in only his second year in the series, he won three times in Busch Grand National racing and every victory was a big one. His pair of wins at Charlotte and the one at Atlanta were all big money victories earned against the best cars and drivers. The first Charlotte win brought home the biggest payday ever in Busch Grand National competition, more than $113,000, because Gordon won the race from the pole and the big bonus that went with it. Gordon's 11 1992 Busch poles broke an all-time record that had been set by no less than Sam Ard.

Winning races and breaking records are part of Gordon's portfolio. Before he retired from almost all open-wheel racing at a youthful 20, Jeff Gordon had won the 1991 USAC Silver Crown (dirt car) championship, becoming the youngest driver in history to do so. In 1991, he won two of the seven races on the series. In 1990, at 19, he became the youngest midget champion in USAC history. When he quit racing midgets, Gordon had won a dozen USAC feature races. Some guys race USAC midgets for an entire career and don't come close to that record.

He could have had any open-wheel ride he wanted, except perhaps at Indianapolis, and even that might not have been out of the question. That's because no matter where he went, no matter if it was dirt or pavement, no matter if he had even seen the car or the track before, Jeff Gordon proved he could win. Credentials like his are as rare as an open seat in the Winston Tower at the Daytona 500. Anyone with credentials like Gordon's could get a top ride, even now, even without a sponsor pushing two fat fists full of money at a car owner.

Examples of his success are everywhere. In 1990, he went to what is arguably the most prestigious midget race in the country, the Belleville Nationals. The Belleville track is a frightening joint, round and with high banks, a short guardrail, a tacky surface, and no margin for error. Belleville crashes are extraordinarily violent, exponentially more devastating than even midget drivers experience on other high-speed tracks. Although he'd never even seen the track before, much less raced on it, Jeff Gordon blew everyone away and won a solid victory in the only appearance he ever made there.

At Phoenix, he kicked butt in his Silver Crown car. The prospect of driving a Silver Crown car on a mile track has made more than a few veteran wheelmen unable to eat on race day, their stomachs so nauseated they empty whole jars of Rolaids. But Jeff Gordon smiles at places like these. Gordon's 1991 season in those fearsome open-wheel cars began at Phoenix, where he won.

So, here's this kid, at least in years, who has come to stock car racing against a background of winning races and championships at a younger age than anyone else. His wins have come at the most frightening tracks, in the most evil cars, and with the best drivers of the day in the field. He's won big races when he's been the least experienced driver on the track. Sometimes, he hasn't even seen the playing field before he beats the best on it.

At an age when his contemporaries were mostly worried about which brand of sneaker was in or what the blonde down the street might say if asked out, Jeff Gordon was busy making himself into a national race car driving champion.

Jeff Gordon got where he is today by starting young, racing hard, and racing well. He's on the way here to winning the Hulman Classic at the one-mile Indiana State Fairgrounds in 1991.
SCR Archives

In one of his first races ever, 13-year-old Jeff Gordon finds himself in the middle of a three-way battle with one of the sport's best, Rich Vogler (15), applying the pressure. *SCR Archives*

Jeff Gordon was raised to be a race car driver. His family didn't force racing on him. They presented the opportunity and their enthusiastic youngster accepted. Gordon's career developed out of a unique set of circumstances that couldn't happen again.

When he was a year old, Gordon's mother and biological father divorced. His mother then married John Bickford, who was involved in racing as a car builder and parts supplier. Gordon says his stepfather steered him toward racing because he was "running crazy, probably driving them [his parents] crazy because I was always on either a bicycle or a skateboard." So, his activity was channeled. "I started racing bicycles when I was just over four. We had a BMX track not far from where we lived [Vallejo, California], and I would ride up there and play around on the jumps. The next thing I knew, I had a pretty tricked-out bike and started racing."

When Gordon was only four and a half, John Bickford pulled into the yard with a trailer carrying a pair of quarter midgets, a pink one for Gordon's sister, Kim, and a black one for Jeff. "She wasn't interested at all, but I was," Gordon remembers. "We made our own track and just basically had fun. Then, we found a racetrack we could go to, a little dirt track. Then we were racing. The next thing I knew we were racing every single weekend."

Gordon vividly recalls his childhood passion for racing. "I had a blast with it. Once I got more experience, I stopped spinning out. Then I started winning. When you start winning, it gives the desire to keep going back."

He moved up and kept winning. "The competition got tougher and the races started getting harder to win. But we kept on winning. We were so competitive and we won a lot. That was what made it so much fun."

At age nine, he raced a 100-cc kart for the first time. The race was a major IKF event with a field full of veterans. He won. "That's when we realized he had a certain knack for getting through a corner," his stepfather explains, "because everyone [in karting] has the same technology, the same horsepower, so they all go down the straightaways the same." He just seemed to have something about him that helped him get through the corners, Bickford added.

In the nine years Gordon raced quarter midgets and karts, his attention turned elsewhere only once. "I got tired of racing every weekend, of practicing during the week," he explains. After all, he was only a kid. In place of racing, "We got a ski boat and the next thing I knew, I was turning into a professional water-skier, going to water-ski school."

But Gordon and his stepfather both missed racing. It was hard to return, however, because Gordon was too old for quarter midgets but not old enough for the next step.

He was just 13. "That's when we were buying a sprint car," he remembers with a twisted smile.

Three years before Jeff could legally drive on the road, Gordon's stepfather bought him a sprinter, the most take-your-head-off dangerous bundle of pent-up violence in motorsports. How could a kid go from water-skiing and quarter midgets to sprinters—and do it at an age when he's not old enough to enter the pits?

Gordon didn't think it was possible. "I didn't think anybody would let me," he says. "Plus, I didn't think I was ready for it. A big 600- to 700-horsepower car.

"I'd heard about Sport Allen [another teenager who was racing sprint cars], I think through *Open Wheel* magazine. He was 14 or 15 at the time. Through the quarter midgets, we became good friends with Robbie Stanley. I think he was 16 or 17 when he started racing sprint cars."

If someone else could do it, Gordon could do it.

"So, we went to Indiana and met Lee Osborne." Osborne, an ex-sprint car racer, a first-class driver who one day put his helmet in the bag for the last time and began building sprint cars for other people, is a worldly fellow. His first reaction to Gordon and Bickford's request for a car was to think he misunderstood that it would be for the 13-year-old. When he realized he'd got it right, Osborne tried to talk them out of it. "He thought we were crazy, but he still built us a race car," says Gordon, whose smile increases in frequency and enthusiasm as the story goes on. "The next thing I knew, we were in Florida, racing at Jacksonville."

It is almost incomprehensible that a 13-year-old kid could drive a sprint car at all since driving a sprint car is about as difficult as flying an air force fighter jet or piloting a submarine. And it's far more dangerous than either. Jeff Gordon certainly wasn't ready for it.

"The first time I sat in the seat, I started it," he remembers. Firing a sprint car engine is difficult because there's no clutch or starter motor. The car is direct drive. The driver locks the gearbox into high, a truck pushes the car off, and at around 30 miles per hour the ignition is turned on firing the engine. From there, the car is in high gear and running.

Gordon remembers his first sprint car experience as a terrorizing affair. "We wanted to make sure I could at least start the thing," before going to Florida. "That was the scariest, most frightening day I've ever had. We were on a gravel road. I didn't know what to expect. So it was real scary."

But he started the car.

John Bickford says he "absolutely" would not have put Gordon in a sprint car at age 13 if he had it to do over again. There was, at the time, no place else a kid between age 13 and 16 could race, and that's how he rationalized the decision at the time. "You're at an age with absolutely nothing to do," Bickford says. Racing had been the family's life and trying to avoid a three-year waiting period as Gordon's birth certificate matured just wasn't acceptable.

Bickford rationalizes the danger he put his stepson face to face with when he talks about how sprint cars are safer than they once were. And, he says putting a 13-year-old kid with zero experience on a track with the best in the business was a "safer" way to do it. "You notice I didn't go to a low-ball race-track. I went with the very best guys. The safest place is the most professional surroundings. I wouldn't even consider taking him to a local track to start sprint car racing."

The first time he drove a sprint car, Gordon raced with the best: Jack Hewitt, Brad Doty, Kelly Kinser. "They know about the mind deal and they told him what to watch out for," Bickford explained.

Still, it wasn't easy. At Jacksonville, rain was coming as Gordon took his first few laps in that sprint car. Bickford remembers, "He clipped the fence. He didn't really hurt the car any. He straightened the car, picked up the throttle, didn't let the front end get into the wall, didn't do anything stupid, and he brought the car around.

"Brad [Doty, an experienced driver] came around and said, 'I don't believe you pulled that off. Fifty percent of the guys here would have spun out, crashed, there'd have been a helluva crash, but you did exactly what any veteran sprint car driver would have done. You got back on the gas, got up to speed, didn't let anyone run over your tires.' "

Gordon's now 16 and a full-blown sprint car driver. He could barely grow a mustache, but he sure could drive a race car.
SCR Archives

Gordon was not as favorably impressed as Brad Doty was. Bickford remembers, "Jeff told me, 'There's no way I can do this.'

"He went into the trailer and told me we're going home. 'You're crazy. You told me this was a lot like racin' a quarter midget. You're nuts. You lied to me.'"

Bickford told Gordon to calm down. He decided to not practice for the next race, East Bay. Instead, he threw Gordon directly into the fire again. This was a series, and instead of a one-car practice, they'd race. The family had towed through terrible weather, an awful drive of sleet, freezing rain, and snow to come to Florida, so they'd race. Bickford remembers that at East Bay, the next stop, Jeff "was like forty-eighth quick. The next night, he was like twenty-eighth quick. The next he was twelfth quick. Once he did OK and got over being a little embarrassed, he really looked pretty good on the track. He used his head."

Gordon says he "got over" being afraid of sprint cars. "It just started clicking—getting over the scary feeling of the horsepower, how light the car was compared to the horsepower, and knowing the car was going to stick when I threw it into the corner. Once I got over that, there was nothing that was going to stop us."

Although his stepfather remembers, Gordon says he doesn't recall ever being so terrified that he wanted to quit racing. "I don't know what it was inside of me telling me that I wanted to do this," he says. "I was nervous and I was scared, but I've always been like that. Each time I moved up in class, I was the same way. I had this nervous feeling. But once I got in it, everything turned out all right."

So, at age 13½, Jeff Gordon found himself racing sprint cars. It was a high-intensity young life, one very different from other kids his age. During the school year, he attended classes. In the summer, he raced all over Indiana and Ohio, where the best sprint races are run. "A couple of my good friends went to the races with me and they thought it was great. But they didn't know how serious I was about racing until I was in high school and a couple of them saw me on TV."

Despite his obsession with race cars, Gordon "was never allowed to take a shop course," says Bickford. "I told him, I said my shop could outdo any shop in the United States. I could teach him more in two hours than any shop teacher could teach him in a whole semester."

This was no idle boast. During high school, Gordon earned extra money fabricating sprint car pieces for Shirley Kears. His folks put some of the money away and spent some of it on an old six-cylinder truck that he and Bickford worked up together.

As for academics, Gordon says he was an average student, "but every time I did something on racing in school, it was As all the time." He graduated with honors as he simultaneously created a racing career.

Indeed, he got all As in racing. If there had been fear early, it was gone by the time Gordon reached his 17th birthday. At 17, he was racing on the fearsome high hills of Eldora in Ohio and other places that have caused some drivers to lose their lunch before a race and others to lose their lives during it.

The first time Gordon ever saw the fearsome Belleville High Banks, he set a new track record, for which he's receiving his award here, and won the biggest race of the year. *SCR Archives*

Progress was linear. Gordon was a quick study, an exceptionally dedicated professional for any age.

Because of his unique situation, more people were willing to help Jeff Gordon than others. Larry Nuber, at the time a major force at ESPN; Jack Hewitt, a top sprint car driver; and Bob East, a chassis builder, all reached out a helping hand. And this kid asked for help. He wanted it, begged for it. Before he was 20 years old, Jeff Gordon had called the major players at every major car company in America looking for their help. But, first, it was racing people who lifted his career, not Detroit's car guys. Help from Detroit would come later.

Among the racing people to spot Gordon's talent was Bob East, who built midgets and who worked with John Bickford. East connected Gordon with a winning car owner, Rollie Helmling, and the connection brought success almost immediately.

The relationship began when Gordon went to a midget race. He remembers watching Helmling's car "running real fast and at the end of the night, they throw the checkered flag and, boom, here goes this car flipping, sliding down the straightaway. Well, it's Helmling's car and it just destroyed the thing." East offered to build a new car for Helmling and suggested putting Gordon behind the wheel to replace the driver who'd tested the roll cage.

"He had no idea of who I was," says Gordon. "John Bickford helped build the car. The result was, well, unbelievable."

The first time Jeff Gordon ever drove a midget was for Helmling at the Night Before the 500 program at IRP. That race is one of the biggest of the year and draws all the hot dogs, the superstars who race their brains out hoping some Indy car owner is in the stands shopping for his next driver.

"We go out," Gordon remembers, "and, bang, it was like miracle night. What nobody, including myself, thought was going to happen is what did happen. Fast time. Track record. Lead halfway. Win the race. And that was the turning point. To win at IRP is a really, really big deal."

It is.

From there, Gordon was hell on wheels. A new sprint car deal was created and he became a TV star.

ESPN's *Saturday Night Thunder*, Gordon will tell you, was yet another of those vital elements, another piece without which he might still be racing sprint cars in Indiana. He ran in the top five at nearly every *Saturday Night Thunder* race that summer and the whole world saw it on TV. It didn't matter whether it was in a sprint car, a Silver Crown car, or a midget, he won. "It was unbelievable," says Gordon in a moment of profound understatement.

Gordon drove Bill Davis' Baby Ruth–sponsored BGN Thunderbird to three wins. He's pictured here at IRP. *SCR Archives*

"I think I won five out of nine or ten TV races. It got me in front of the camera. Got me working with sponsors. I'd driven a lot of cars, a lot of tracks, but the TV series was definitely the turning point of my career."

But even when he wasn't on TV, Gordon was winning races. Sprints, midgets, champ cars, it didn't matter. Gordon just slid behind the wheel, fastened his seatbelt and shortly thereafter smiled for the victory lane photographers. And we're talking major league races here. These were big races with big names. "There was a momentum period where I had a lot of confidence in myself and the guys I was driving for, and I think they had a lot of confidence in me. Everywhere we went, we were the guys to beat," he remembers.

Gordon isn't bragging. He's telling the story exactly as it happened. It's the way it was. And perhaps that's the way it will be in the future, in Winston Cup.

"It still goes back to the same thing here [stock cars]," he says. "When you have momentum, confidence, and everything is clicking, you're unbeatable. I didn't know why things were going so well for me, but I didn't want it to stop."

As Gordon's career continues to unfold, the clicking sound grows louder and more intense.

It is not preposterous to consider Gordon the greatest talent to hit big time stock car racing since Richard Petty. Just look at what he's done in open-wheel racing. Then look closely at his first few attempts in a stock car.

Gordon's stock car career began at the Buck Baker driving school, where he went to see if he liked heavy cars that race at high speed on narrow tires. There was good reason to find out: Gordon had never driven a Busch or Winston Cup stock car and had been offered a spot with Toyota's stadium truck racing program. "I didn't know what I wanted to do," Gordon remembers. "Things were going really, really well with the midgets and sprint cars, and I knew the momentum was behind me and I had an opportunity to move on."

He just didn't know where to move to.

At Baker's school, Gordon met Hugh Connerty, who raced his own Busch Grand National car on-and-off. Baker, who was impressed with Gordon, talked Connerty into giving the youngster a chance to drive the car at the school. "I made ten laps, did well, and we went out to dinner," Gordon remembers. They talked and Connerty offered Gordon the chance to drive in a few races. But he had to come up with some money to get the ride.

Gordon called everyone he'd ever heard of that might help, but he got no further than a few product deals. The team landed a small restaurant sponsorship and Gordon went to Charlotte to run an open practice. "We went really fast," he remembers. "The car was good. It took me two days to get up to speed, but by the second day we were running speeds that were good enough for maybe tenth qualifying position. So, we got an OK [from NASCAR] to race."

Gordon drove the Outback Steakhouse car in his first Busch attempt. The car and team were not the best and not much should have been expected of a rookie driver. In his first qualifying attempt in the series, at Rockingham, Gordon put the Outback car out front: on the outside pole to be exact. The race was less pleasing as he only went 40 laps before the car, which was too loose, got the best of its driver and the day ended in the wall.

But more good came of that Rockingham run than just starting on the outside of the front row.

Jeff Gordon earned the attention of Ford's Lee Morse. "I think it was about two weeks, maybe three, after that race when he called," says Gordon. "I'm talking to Lee and he says, 'Would you be interested in the [Bill Davis] Carolina Ford Dealers car?' Excuse me? What? Every race I'd been to, that car flew."

Morse connected Gordon and Bill Davis. The deal was that Hugh Connerty and Davis were to merge, with Connerty serving as sponsor finder. Gordon would drive, and Davis would prepare the cars. But Connerty couldn't find a sponsor, so he was out. Gordon and Davis went to Rockingham to test tires for Goodyear and Gordon remembers, "a few other teams were there and it was the first time I had met or even seen any of the guys on Davis' team. We flew. The car was a rocket. It was the best-feeling car I'd ever had. I think we were the quickest car there. It was just a match made in heaven from there."

Instead of racing trucks in stadiums, Gordon decided to drive stock cars for Bill Davis.

Gordon's deal was for 15 races in 1991, sponsor or no sponsor, but 15 races isn't the way it worked out. "We got eight or ten races into the season," says Gordon now with as broad a grin as he can accomplish. "We were spinning out every race, but we were finishing every race." Not only were they finishing, but Gordon put Davis' car up front on several occasions. Davis was sufficiently impressed, and he committed to run every event, sponsor or no sponsor.

The team didn't win in its rookie season, but it finished second three times and ran up front often.

And then came 1992. With Bill Davis, Gordon scored 3 big wins, 11 poles. And he got an invitation from Rick Hendrick to go Winston Cup.

Ask Bill Davis and he'll tell you it was well understood that he and Gordon, together with Ford's help and blessing, would race Winston Cup in 1993. Maybe not a full schedule, well, maybe a full schedule, but definitely Winston Cup. Then, on the eve of the Memorial Day race at Charlotte, Gordon told Davis he'd finish the 1992 season with him, but that's it. He'd signed with Hendrick.

Davis probably would have felt better if Gordon had hit him in the stomach with a baseball bat.

Gordon, with a full appreciation of Hendrick's abundant resources and that Davis hadn't run a lap of Winston Cup, never gave Davis a chance to counter offer. He had negotiated only with Hendrick. Davis never knew what was happening, never guessed Gordon was contemplating leaving until it was over.

Davis was devastated. "We were like family," he said. Days later, at Charlotte, the press interviewed Bill Davis, who told them how hurt he was. Davis, as gentle and nice a guy as ever owned a race car, got all the sympathy. Gordon was hammered in the press.

National Speed Sport News' May 13th edition headlined, "Gordon Move Jolts Ford." Ford's Michael Kranefuss was quoted in the paper saying, "As far as I'm concerned, he doesn't need to worry about Ford anymore." Kranefuss was hurt and said, "We put him in Grand National, we invested a lot of money, made sure he got all the right people, so why would he all of a sudden treat us like a piece of s—?"

Davis said he was "barely speaking" to Gordon at the Charlotte race. The tension in the pit was as visible as the speed of the car. All weekend long, Gordon answered the same questions. Reporters and fans wanted

One of Gordon's biggest stock car wins came at Charlotte in May 1992, when he took home the biggest payoff ever won by a Busch Grand National driver. Just two weeks before, he jolted racing and his team by signing to race Winston Cup for Rick Hendrick. *SCR Archives*

to know what kind of guy would leave "family" and go race somewhere else. And in a Chevrolet, no less, after Ford had put him where he was. Through it all, Gordon stayed cool and never complained about the press he got even though it was decidedly one-sided. Saddam Hussein might have been treated better.

Gordon just put it all out of his mind when it came time to go to work. He put the car on the pole and won the race. Later, he explained, "When I get into that race car, things on my mind are gone. It's time to drive the race car to the best of my ability. My mind's not on this deal or that deal or on turmoil."

Gordon handled the bad press with quiet dignity and without a single complaint. Nobody seemed as much interested in the fact that a 20-year-old had just signed with a top Winston Cup team as they were about a young man who had turned his back on his benefactors. The young man let it happen without re-action until now.

Upon reflection, Gordon says, "It was unfortunate the way things happened." He would have done it differently, if he could go back and do it again, because "we had become, I mean, he [was] basically my boss and we became really good friends and that made it really tough. I had to make a decision for Jeff Gordon and if Bill Davis had to make a decision for Bill Davis and it excluded me, I think we would have been in the opposite situation. It was tough because we became good friends.

"This is a business and when you get to this level, you have to make decisions that sometimes hurt people's feelings."

It was also tough because Davis had been around longer and had the sympathy of everyone in the garage. If there's anyone in Busch racing who is well liked, it's Bill Davis. They hardly knew the kid who came from sprint car racing.

The stories said Gordon's decision was motivated by money. Gordon says the stories were wrong. "I felt it was pretty unfair to me." There were reports of millions of dollars involved in the deal. Some of those reports claimed Gordon got a million up front. Gordon says money wasn't an issue. Racing and his chance to be successful at it was the only issue. He said he didn't even talk to Hendrick about money until he received the written contract, which included financial terms. What he did talk about, what he negotiated was "Ray Evernham. That was my first question. Because Ray Evernham and I have some magic together."

Evernham is a mechanical genius who as a driver won a bunch of modified stock car races and once was shop foreman at IROC. He is as good with the mechanical end of cars and race strategy as Jeff Gordon is at driving. To use Gordon's phrase, these guys click.

When Evernham quit driving race cars after a couple of serious jingles with the steel wall at the Flemington Speedway, he went to work for Bill Davis and when he did, Jeff Gordon started winning both poles and races.

After the bombshell announcement of Gordon's move to Hendrick, and that he was taking Evernham with him to be team manager, that was the end of Ray Evernham and Bill Davis Racing. It was also the end of Jeff Gordon winning until Charlotte in October. In an extraordinary move of sportsmanship, Hendrick loaned Ray Evernham to Davis for one weekend. It was a good move because with Gordon at the wheel and Evernham plotting strategy with Davis and Elton Sawyer, the team won the pole, led at the halfway point, and won the race. Again.

Getting Ray Evernham on the team at Hendrick was, for Gordon, much more important than getting a salary of a million dollars a year. Gordon says he and Evernham "always talked about the perfect deal. To be able to hire the people we want. We wanted to know where the cars were going to come from. Were we going to be a third-class team or a number-one team in a three-team field? I had basically made my decision after our second or third meeting [with Hendrick and his people] and that was before dollars were even, I mean, we never talked about money."

The plan is that in 1993 Rick Hendrick will have three number-one cars. The teams will share information and equipment.

"We're going to get what Ricky Rudd and Kenny Schrader get," Gordon explains. "That's one thing that's really big about Rick Hendrick—all three teams, none of them overrides the other. I mean, it's whatever it takes to win.

"I don't think there's going to be any team out there that's going to have any better equipment."

But it takes more than equipment to win races and Gordon doesn't expect to be the champion in his first year. "We're not going to come out of the box and start kicking everybody's butt," he says. "We're working on the future."

Gordon doesn't want to be the next Tim Richmond. Or the next Richard Petty. "I want to be the next Jeff Gordon," he explains. "I want to make a name for myself. I want to win races, to be in Winston Cup for a long, long time."

All of his focus is on racing.

He is single, and although there's a girl-friend who lives in Indiana, racing is first. "I don't see her very often," he says. "With my lifestyle in racing, I'm a very busy person. Racing is it. Racing is first. Women are further down the list."

It's 1991 and, as hard as it seems to believe, the young team of Bill Davis and Jeff Gordon was struggling with no year-long sponsor and lots of growing pains. They got over both problems in a big way in 1992.
SCR Archives

For fun, Gordon likes to be around racing. He jet-skis, goes to concerts, works out, and plays some racquetball. He washes his own clothes and writes his own checks to pay his own bills. He lives in a home he shares with two other men and says the stories about the beautiful women who call, wanting to spend time with a soon-to-be-wealthy and winning Winston Cup driver are just an illusion, someone else's fantasy. He says his life isn't so glamorous.

Yet he is very aware that his life will change in 1993, that he'll sign his autograph more often than most people take a breath. "I know what it's going to take," he says. "You have to be nice to every person that walks up to you. You have to do interviews. I feel like I'm prepared and I'm looking forward to it.

"Right now, the way things are going for me, I wouldn't want to change anything in the world. There's a million people that would like to be in my seat, where I'm at, and I'm happy where I'm at. I want to work as hard as I possibly can to make sure that things keep going the way they are."

THE NEW TALENT

Although it seems entirely self-evident that Jeff Gordon has enormous talent, neither he nor his stepfather, who has guided his career, will admit it.

John Bickford explains that success in racing comes not just from a driver's ability, good engines, a great mechanic, luck, or dedication. All those thing must combine into a package, Bickford says.

He explains, "I think what Jeff has that's unique is not a physical ability, it is a great package. All the winners you see around the world, in every form of racing, they have great packages. It's not one thing a driver carries. Although the driver may move from place to place, it's the package" that counts.

"If you analyze his career, you'll see that the places where Jeff hasn't been especially successful, he doesn't stay very long. We don't try to explain it. The package wasn't complete. There was an end of the box that was open and we had to readjust to close up the box so we could make the package complete.

"That happened to us a couple of times in sprint car racing. If you don't have the motors...there's no way you're gonna compete. We felt the package was always the thing. Keep the people around you. Keep the package."

Ray Evernham, who will captain Gordon's team in 1993, has a different view of Gordon. "Every time we go somewhere, he amazes me. He put not only me in awe at our first test [in a Winston Cup car] but all the people from Chevrolet who were there. These people from Chevrolet, in five laps they were looking at their stopwatches and shaking their heads. The fifth lap he ever made in a Winston Cup car was fast enough to put him in the top ten in qualifying. Later, he had a lap down there that was faster than the track record. It was just amazing."

Yet Bickford does identify something special Jeff Gordon brings to any race. "The thing about Jeff," Bickford explains, "is he got [Steve] Kinser's relentless desire to do good. It don't matter how far down he gets. He never gives up. You don't ever count him out.

"Ya have to be relentless. Things change. The track can come to you."

Bickford says his stepson is "exceptionally smart. I don't know what his IQ is, but he's real smart.

"When you are the smartest guy, you are also the fastest guy."

Ask Jeff Gordon about his success and his talent. There's no snap answer although the question has been asked before. He searches his mind and begins a list of good cars, good advice he's gotten and followed. "I didn't think I had anything special," he says. "I still don't. I think there's a lot of people out there that can drive race cars as good as me. One thing I do have over a lot of people is experience in the type of racing I've done at such a young age.

"Mom and dad had a lot to do with that but I honestly don't know why I've gotten to this level. I don't think there was any magical thing that we did that got me here, any talent I have over anyone else. No, I don't think I had any special talent. There were a hundred guys out there racing sprint cars blowing my doors off."

Evernham doesn't remember any sprint car doors flying through the air. He says, "[Jeff] is a natural. Two years ago in your magazine, I said he reminded me of Al Unser Jr. I thought they were the two most naturally talented drivers I'd ever seen. But now I'm beginning to wonder. I don't think anyone has any idea how good this kid really is. I think I'm good about setting up a car. But I'm not that good. I don't know how he does it. He's got some feel."

John Bickford's thinking about working within a proper package has imprinted on Jeff Gordon, who says, "What dawned on me was that being in good equipment and being around good people, with the people who were helping me, we were all kind of exceptional. I don't think I could have done it without them or that they could have done it without me.

"Every time I've been successful or not I go back to that theory.

"I've been down in the ditch before where things weren't going my way and I look back and I know why things didn't click. I moved on and I got hooked up with some good people and, boom, things start clicking again."

Jeff Gordon listens to John Bickford Sr. at a midget race in 1989. *SCR Archives*

THE COCA-COLA 600: JEFF'S FIRST CUP WIN

BY BENNY PHILLIPS
Stock Car Racing, September, 1994

There Will Be Many More

When Jeff Gordon came off the fourth turn the final time and looked down the straight-away, whether he realized it or not, it was the beginning of his chase of Petty, Pearson, Yarborough, Allison, and Earnhardt.

As he looked toward the checkered flag, he saw the same view as great drivers of bygone moments. They smelled the same smoking tires, the same hot engines, and for brief moments their pulses were quickened by the

A young and emotional Gordon fought back tears at his first Winston Cup win at Charlotte Motor Speedway (CMS) in 1994. *SCR Archives*

same packed grandstand of waving and cheering fans.

So, for purposes related to the future, Gordon's career began on the night of the 1994 Coke 600 at Charlotte Motor Speedway. It was his first Winston Cup points victory (he had previously won a 125-mile Daytona qualifier, the Winston Select Open, and the Busch Clash), and the exact hour he began pursuing the records of immortals.

Racing is really too young to be sure of its names with lasting fame—such as baseball's Ruth, football's Grange, and boxing's Louis—but we believe it fair to say Richard Petty's name (not Petty, but Richard Petty), David Pearson's name, Cale Yarborough's name, Bobby Allison's name, and Dale Earnhardt's name will exempt oblivion.

For 15 months on the Winston Cup circuit, Gordon had been trying to be the best he could be, rather than the best anyone has ever been, which at times seemed to be what folks expected. From the very moment he came on the circuit, he had been looked upon by some as stock car racing's next superstar.

Some of it had to do with his previous racing experience. He had always been a winner. He tossed in his chips with Ford and the Grand National ranks and strolled into the Chevrolet and Winston Cup ranks in 1993. He broke the slats on his crib at 21 and became the youngest driver to win a 125-mile qualifying race at Daytona. He diced with Earnhardt and Dale Jarrett for the lead in the latter stages of the Daytona 500 that followed, and he was on his way to becoming rookie of the year. He finished second to Earnhardt a year ago in the 600 and was second to Ricky Rudd at Michigan.

Then he smoked the field in this year's Busch Clash at Daytona.

All this set the stage for Charlotte and victory in the Coca-Cola 600. It was an emotional time for Gordon and crew chief Ray Evernham, the one-two package for Rick Hendrick Motorsports.

The victory came with daring moves that caught opponents by surprise. On a night when tires were disintegrating and drivers were more than mildly concerned, Evernham made an adventurous call that led to Gordon's first victory.

After watching all his rivals take four tires during their last runs down pit road in the final 25 laps, Evernham wagered that Gordon could hold on to the lead with just two new tires.

That is what he did with 18 laps to go with only right-side tires. It was a 9.5-second stop, and put Gordon back on the track in second place, behind Ricky Rudd, who still had to stop for fuel. When Rudd pitted on lap 391, Gordon took command and led the final nine laps, finishing nearly four seconds ahead of Rusty Wallace. Geoff Bodine came in third, Jarrett fourth, and Ernie Irvan rounded out the top five.

Evernham's decision caught competitors by surprise. Wallace, who led 187 of the 400 laps, held a slight edge on the field when he pitted on lap 375. He took on four tires and fuel and was out of the pits in 16.5 seconds. Geoff Bodine, four seconds behind Wallace when pit stops began, pitted a few laps after the leader. He took four tires and fuel, and was out in 17.9 seconds.

Gordon's stop put him out four seconds ahead of Wallace, a margin he managed to hold. After the stop, Evernham left it up to Gordon, who handled it well . . . Well, up until the end.

Gordon didn't immediately conquer CMS, as this wadded up No. 24 shows.
SCR Archives

Above: Gordon and Evernham discuss their car's setup at Bristol in 1996. He finished first and second in the two races there that season. *SCR Archives*

Right: The elusive "chemistry" between driver and crew chief was almost immediate between Gordon and Evernham. *SCR Archives*

"Ray was in the pits saying, 'Come on, buddy, this is your race.

You can win this thing. Push it hard, push it hard.' "

He saw the white flag wave, the signal that if all went well in the next 30 seconds, four turns, and 1.5 miles, he would win the race, a rather awesome achievement for a driver in just his second year on the circuit. As he watched the waving white flag, he suddenly could not see his way clearly.

"I was trying to keep from running into the wall . . . with tears coming down," Gordon says. "I saw the white flag and then when I crossed the line, I just lost it. Dale Earnhardt and some others pulled up beside me to congratulate me and at first I didn't realize who they were."

Everybody loves a winner. Jeff Gordon is a lovable winner. Nothing casual or nonchalant about this guy or his enthusiasm for life. And though he has been racing since almost before he could walk and though he has won hundreds of races in everything from midgets and sprints to Grand National stock cars, this is his first points win in the profession he has chosen as his life's work.

"I knew I couldn't make a mistake," says Gordon, who averaged 139.445 miles per hour and won $200,000.

"With ten to go, I was looking in my mirror every single corner, every single lap. I tried to put a little distance between us. I pretty much knew with ten to go it was ours, and I started choking up. I said, 'Hey, I can't think about that. I've got to focus.'

"So, I was hanging it out for all it was worth," Gordon says. "You've got to know when to be patient and when to be aggressive, and right then was the time to be very aggressive because I had no idea how many laps it was going to take for those guys to catch me."

Gordon says if he never won another race, he would be happy with his life and his career.

Naïve, perhaps, but so refreshing is this kid full of talent who wields such a heavy stick.

Gordon adds that he had nothing to do with the call. Instead Evernham made it, and Evernham says the call actually wasn't too hard.

"We were paying attention to our stopwatches, and Jeff was running pretty easy," Evernham says. "We were looking at Rusty. We were thinking about gas and go. But I'd been thinking about two tires. When they [Rusty] took four, that made it pretty easy for us.

"I didn't let anybody know because everybody has scanners. When Jeff came down pit road, I yelled, 'Two tires, two tires.' And there were some pretty big eyes when our guys went over the wall."

Evernham says he had two or three different plans as to what he was going to do. "We were going to see how the stopwatches showed what Jeff was doing. We were watching Rusty's gas stops and figured he would probably have to come in about lap 380.

"I really had my heart on taking just two tires. I felt if we took four, the car might get too tight."

Evernham says Charlotte Motor Speedway is Gordon's nest. "We do well here, and it was our night. We knew Jeff would have his hands full during daylight hours. We wanted him to be patient. I told him when the sun went down, the track would come to him."

The race started at 5 p.m., and ended under the lights.

Gordon said his car was junk in the final practice Saturday afternoon. "It wasn't doing anything right, but Ray kept telling me it would be OK on Sunday after the sun went down."

At the start of the 600, track temperature was 122 degrees, and at the finish it was 87 degrees.

Gordon's car was junk too; the previous Saturday night he was involved in a wreck during the running of the Winston Select. He ran well enough in the Winston Open to make the main event, and then was involved in a multi-car crash.

"We have several cars at the shop," Gordon said Wednesday night after winning pole position for the 600, "but this is the car we feel is best suited for racing at Charlotte.

"We carried the car back to the shop after the Winston and began working on it almost immediately. The crew worked in shifts, everybody working on it all the time. The car was completed about two a.m. today."

Gordon's speeds were noticeably quicker the night leading up to the race. "They should name that car Sundown," Terry Labonte, Gordon's teammate, said on the eve of the 600. "It hardly runs out of its shadow when the sun is out, but once that sun goes behind those grandstands over there, the car begins to fly."

Until final stops, Wallace and Bodine were the story of the race. Wallace led 187 laps and Bodine 101. Rick Mast led 46 laps, Ernie Irvan 23, Gordon 16 in all, Rudd 10, Dale Jarrett 9, and Ken Schrader 8.

There were 9 caution flags for 46 laps, and a couple of spectacular accidents. The first involved cars driven by Mark Martin, Kyle Petty, Mast, Earnhardt, Bill Elliott, Darrell Waltrip, Ward Burton, John Andretti, and Dick Trickle.

It happened three laps after a restart. Martin came down the backstretch in the middle of a pack, his left rear tire tearing apart. He signaled he was in trouble and tried to move to the inside of the track, but Earnhardt tagged him in the rear and sent him spinning. The other cars piled in. The wreck took out Martin, Trickle, Burton, and Andretti.

Labonte also had a tire tear to pieces. He spun off turn four. Harry Gant and Derrike Cope were also involved.

Bobby Labonte slowed and was headed for the pits. Brett Bodine, with the sun in his face, didn't see Labonte and drove into the rear of his car.

Labonte was surprised at getting hit from behind, and Wallace was surprised at getting hit between the eyes with Evernham's pit-stop venture.

"It was a chancy move to put just two tires on," Wallace says. "We really had 'em beat bad, and I never thought anyone would try just two tires. And I never thought it would work. I guess, looking back, we should have changed two, and we would have won by a ton. There is no doubt we had the strongest car all day, but it was a pretty savvy move on their part."

Buddy Parrott, Wallace's crew chief, says he called for a four-tire stop, and did not even think about Gordon.

"We wanted to make sure Goodyear won the race," Parrott says. "We wanted to be sure we beat Geoff Bodine. He was on Hoosier tires. I didn't figure Gordon was in the hunt."

Bodine, the only Hoosier driver still in the chase at the end, was neck and neck with Wallace when the leaders began making final pit stops. When Wallace, half a second ahead of Bodine before pitting, came out with a four and a half second lead, the race appeared to be his.

Gordon's fabled car control was honed in sprint cars on tracks across the United States as he became the '79 and '81 quarter midget champ; the '90 USAC midget champ; and the '91 USAC Silver Crown champ. He and crew chief Ray Evernham were able to quickly adapt it to stock cars. *SCR Archives*

Then Evernham made his move.

"We went with four tires and thought that would be quicker," Bodine says. "But Gordon went with two, and he held us off. I can't believe it. I thought for sure Rusty would catch him.

"But that was a good run for us."

Jarrett may have summed it up best. "I'd have to say Gordon outfoxed everybody," he said.

Rudd nearly pulled the stunner of the evening. He gambled on gas mileage to take the lead in the closing laps while the other five men still on the lead lap pitted. Rudd took the lead on lap 383 and held it the next 10 laps, waiting for a yellow that never came.

"The only chance we had was to catch a caution and maybe catch everybody down," Rudd said. "We knew we couldn't make it on fuel, and we knew if you were going to stop and get tires, you had to stop early and take advantage of them. So we came late and made a three-second fuel stop."

How important is the 600? Kyle Petty came in 21st and Felix Sabates, his team owner, fired three members of the crew on Monday, including crew chief Robin Pemberton. Also released were Pemberton's brothers, Roman and Ryan.

BGN rookie Jeff Gordon at speed in turn one at Watkins Glen 1991. He finished sixth.
SCR Archives

Fellow Cup rookies Jeff Gordon and Kenny Wallace talk in the garage area at the Pontiac Excitement 400 at Richmond.
SCR Archives

Several, including Wallace, Bodine, and Rudd, came close to winning the race, but as it turned out, the stunners were Gordon and Evernham. The touch of sadness was Gordon for a brief moment as he recalled an old friend, Robbie Stanley, who was fatally injured the previous week in a sprint car race at Winchester (Indiana) Speedway. Gordon recalled that they had started their racing careers together. It was a friendship, he said, that in recent years had "gone different ways," but Robbie and his family, who helped him in the beginning, were friends he would never forget.

So it was on this night that Jeff Gordon began his career chase of big names in the sport, unknown to any of us where it will end. But for right now big names, and Gordon as well, will just have to settle for being as immortal as mortals can be.

DUPONT COMES UP
A WINNER

DuPont is winning in big league stock car racing. Their entry to the sport with driver Jeff Gordon was an immediate success as Gordon won the second race he ever ran for DuPont, the 1993 125-mile qualifying race preceding the Daytona 500. Since then, Gordon has won two Charlotte poles, the Winston Open, the 1994 Busch Clash, and now the Coke 600, all with DuPont livery.

DuPont's other driver, Ricky Craven, is euqally hot. He finished second in Busch Series points in 1993 in only his second full year on the circuit. This year, by press time he'd already won two events and was atop the points battle in his first year as an owner-operator.

With remarkable perception in selecting two young and as–yet–unproven drivers, DuPont was on its way.

But the story behind the story is what DuPont is doing in big time racing to market its products. A manufacturer of automotive paints and bodywork chemicals, DuPont isn't just running up front, it has found racing to be an excellent test facility for its products.

According to DuPont's Tom Speakman, "We think [NASCAR] is an excellent place to showcase our finishes. What's more visible than a race car going around the track? If a finish can hold up under the conditions of a 500–mile race, the finish on a typical car would never have to withstand the same environment so it's an excellent way to have a very durable product."

Speakman says the biggest threat to a finish's surface in NASCAR is "chipping by whatever is on the track. The grit and gravel. You look at Jeff's [Gordon] car and you'll see it holds up very well. Plus the gas, the chemicals, the countless things the paint has to withstand."

DuPont is also using racing to market automotive paint and bodywork chemicals. The company see its customers sitting in racing's grandstands or watching it on television, so DuPont uses racing as a sales device. Entertainment at events is a big part of the DuPont program. "We probably entertain more than anyone else in NASCAR," says Speakman. "We bring customers who buy our paint to the races through sales promotional programs. There are opportunities to win sales contests. By buying X amount of paint, they earn tickets and hospitality access for a race. When we entertain people [at a NASCAR race], we have the right story to tell and the right product to sell. We think NASCAR is an excellent bridge to get closer with our customer."

Forty different Busch and Winston Cup teams use DuPont paints including those of Sterling Marlin, Ernie Irvan, Bill Elliott, Terry Labonte, and of course Jeff Gordon and

THE RACE THAT MADE JEFF GORDON: THE BRICKYARD 400

STAFF REPORT
Circle Track, December 1994

Winston Cup Analysis

Young driving-sensation Jeff Gordon's flourishing career that accelerated in the glow and glory of victory at Indianapolis Motor Speedway appears destined for future greatness, as predicted, in the NASCAR Winston Cup Series.

In winning the inaugural Brickyard 400 stock car extravaganza, the amazing kid, two days past his 23rd birthday, became The Man, convincingly showcasing before the most witnesses ever to view a NASCAR race that he had the "right stuff" to become the next Dale Earnhardt, or more.

It was a fairy tale for the youngest driver in the event, and for a Hendrick Motorsports/DuPont Chevrolet team that had competed in only 50 Winston Cup events, to win the biggest race in NASCAR history—the only race, other than the Indianapolis 500, at the hallowed Speedway. That demonstrated Gordon's rare talent, his potential for greatness. He either outran or outlasted the best NASCAR has to offer, including the old pros in all the magical black cars, treading on and conquering the unknowns, and overcoming the intimidations of a strange racetrack.

Raw Talent

"Jeff has more raw talent than any race driver I've ever seen," says Rick Hendrick, his team owner. "I think he grew up a long time before the Brickyard 400, but he has matured a lot this year. He is aggressive but more patient. He knows when to race [and] how to win. It's still incredible that we won Indy."

In less than two years, Gordon has streaked toward the top of the motorsports world, but to him his rising star is like a fantasy—one big, overwhelming candy store. So the Disney World "Trip of Champions" as the Brickyard 400 winner was quite fitting. He has a cereal-box face (so Kellogg's obliged), a small body that is 20 pounds lighter than the 165-pound permanent Brickyard 400 trophy, and he seems

Gordon celebrates his second Cup win and the first ever for stock cars at the magical Indianapolis Motor Speedway. His storybook Brickyard 400 win—local Indiana boy wins at the mother church of racetracks—etched him in the record books and in the minds of racing fans everywhere. *SCR Archives*

too fragile to wrestle a 3,500-pound stock car 500 miles. Plus, Gordon has an engaging personality, intelligence, and common sense. His noggin, though crammed with so much so soon, remains the same size.

He has a top ride with the largest and most resourceful Winston Cup operation, a beautiful fiancé—former Miss Winston queen Brooke Sealey at his side [they plan to marry on November 25, 1994]—and mounting riches. Everybody wanted to be Jeff Gordon at Indy. "I admit, I'm jealous," says fellow-driver Michael Waltrip, who finished eighth in the Bahari/Pennzoil Pontiac but was winless in 256 big-league starts. "I wished I were Jeff Gordon on August 6, 1994; that I could have been in his shoes that day. I am also very proud and happy for him."

Perhaps Gordon's most endearing quality is humility—a saving grace for a youthful athlete on the rise. After Ernie Irvan, his most fearsome competitor, fell from contention with a punctured right-front tire on his Robert Yates Racing/Havoline Star Ford, Gordon, less than five laps from triumph, got on the radio and thanked crew chief Ray Evernham, Hendrick, and his relatively young crew for giving him the Chevrolet and the support to win. Then he yelled and screamed and bawled in ecstasy, taking an extra lap because he didn't want to go to victory circle with more than 300,000 people and a national ABC television audience thinking he was a crybaby.

This spectacle was an inspiration to every kid with a dream. Afterward he said that winning the Indianapolis 500 of stock car racing was the greatest thing in the world for him and his team and that the experience defied description.

"There's no way I ever thought I'd be in Winston Cup or racing at Indianapolis," Gordon says. "There were so many steps along the way. Meeting Ray Evernham was one of those giant steps. It's so funny the luck that's on your side or the breaks you get. There are a million kids out there the same age as me who have a lot of talent and don't get the breaks. I hope car owners and sponsors continue to look for those guys and that the kids won't give up until their dreams come true. Who'd have thought I would be racing for Rick Hendrick? [Who'd have thought] that he would give me the opportunity, and that I would be able to do something with it?"

Controlled Aggression

Youth and an aggressive driving style, sometimes too aggressive he says, have made Gordon extremely popular. A new dimension of endearment was added when he won the hearts of Indiana, which he passed through en route to NASCAR. He has adopted the Indianapolis suburb of Pittsboro as his hometown. His victory brought townspeople and the fire engine onto the streets in revelry. He will return to the second Brickyard 400 next August 5, 1994, with an almost certain visit to Pittsboro, as the Hoosier state's newest motorsports darling.

It is only 15 miles from Pittsboro to Indianapolis Motor Speedway, but it was a circuitous, whirlwind 10-year journey for Gordon to get there and to become the first driver to etch his name alongside that of Ray Harroun, the inaugural 500 champion in 1911.

Gordon attended his first 500 in 1983. Eleven at the time, he stood by the garage fence until he got his hero, Rick Mears, to autograph a T-shirt, "To Jeff." His mother has the keepsake. When Gordon was 13, his mother, Carol, and stepfather, John Bickford (who had put his stepson in a kart at age five), decided to move to Indiana, the hub of open-wheel racing, because California required sprint car drivers to be at least 16.

Winning USAC midget and sprint car titles, Gordon groomed himself for Indy cars, but he wanted to try NASCAR stockers and found his niche in the big-time when he hooked up with Hendrick. The first-time Hendrick, who owns a three-team, Charlotte-based Winston Cup stable and 70 auto dealerships in eight states, noticed Gordon was in a NASCAR Busch Grand National race at Atlanta Motor Speedway in early 1992.

Dale Earnhardt gets a jump on pole-sitter Rick Mast and the rest of the field at the start of the first Brickyard 400. *SCR Archives*

"I was climbing the steps to a lounge with some friends," Hendrick says. "This guy was sliding his car with the rear end hanging out almost sideways through the turns. I told my friends, 'Let's watch for a minute, this guy's going to bust his butt.' But he didn't. He did it lap after lap. I'd never seen anybody handle a loose car like that without losing control.

"I didn't know Jeff. I inquired and learned he was a hot prospect. Because he was driving for top BGN-owner Bill Davis, I assumed he was being groomed by Ford Motor Company and was under contract. But I learned that one of my employees was Jeff's roommate, and he said he didn't have a contract. Two days later he did—with me. I couldn't believe Ford hadn't protected him."

Gordon's deal, said to be a four-year pact with a $600,000 annual guarantee, a whopper for a rookie, also included Evernham, his BGN crew chief, in the package. Evernham, a New Jersey modified driver who reluctantly decided he was a better mechanic and leader than driver, led Gordon to three major BGN victories, a record 11 poles, and $412,000 in earnings and top-rookie honors in 1992. They clicked instantly.

Gordon and the newest Hendrick entry did everything but win in their rookie season last year— seven top fives, 11 top 10s, and 14th ranking in points—making Gordon rookie of the year by a landslide.

This year, Gordon prefaced the Brickyard windfall with his first Winston Cup victory in the Coca-Cola 600, a spectacle under the lights at Charlotte Motor Speedway on May 29 (same day as the Indianapolis 500). "I knew Jeff was a winner," Hendrick says. "It was a case of when. Now [it is a case of] how many. Imagine, the kid's only 23 years old."

Gordon is paying his boss' dividends. The $613,000 Brickyard 400 prize, more than double the previous single-race NASCAR payday, sent Gordon's season gross to a series-leading $1,332,395 and his total for 50 races to $2.1 million.

But money wasn't the ruling factor at the Brickyard. "Charlotte was a great thrill, and I wouldn't have wanted my first win to come anywhere else; just like I wouldn't have wanted my second anywhere but Indy," Gordon says. "Charlotte really prepared us for the Brickyard. It relieved a ton of pressure generated by our own high expectations and those of others, and it gave us experience. We got our act together and knew we could win. I don't think a driver who's never won could come to Indy and do what we did."

Equal Track Terms

"There was another major factor," Gordon continues. "The first NASCAR race at Indy put us on equal turf and terms. It's so hard for us to go to some of the tracks our leading competitors have raced on for years and hit [that] combination. Ray is good at that; on equal terms, he's the best. We work well together. Right now we are professionally inseparable and I hope we always are."

Evernham told Gordon before the race, "Kid, everybody's a rookie here. [But] you can be 'the man'." "Indy cars were my love," Evernham says. "I remember the old front-engine roadsters. My dreams were built around driving at Indy, but I realized I wasn't good enough. I choked up pushing our car to the line for the Brickyard 400. It was my second chance at Indy, and most people don't get that.

"I'm living my dreams through Jeff. That little guy has made my professional life and that's the first thing I told him when I finally got to talk with him two days after the race. He's the kind of guy who paid $2,500 to charter an airplane to fly home from an appearance to my son's [Ray J., who has leukemia] third birthday party in July. Jeff gave Ray J. an electric four-wheel-drive truck. Ray got on that thing, took off across the room, and crashed into the wall. Jeff rolled on the floor laughing with tears in his eyes. Jeff is everything I always wanted to be."

And Gordon was everything that Chevrolet and Goodyear wanted him to be. The victory broke a seven-race win binge by Ford, dating to the Coca-Cola 600. In all their glory to that juncture of the season—12 wins and a 15-point lead in the manufacturers' title chase—Ford Motor Company brass undoubtedly grimaced again at having lost Gordon to their archrival.

Goodyear, worried over rival Hoosier Tire's only victory of the season (a runaway at Pocono), prevailed for the 18th time, sweeping the first 17 positions. Though Goodyear dominated with 31 cars in a field of 43, competitors rated the rival tires about equal. But Hoosier's top cars fell out of contention. Hoosier cars started on the pole and fourth; Goodyear machines second and third. "Needless to say, this was a very important victory for Goodyear Eagles," says racing director Leo Mehl. "We ran more than 2,500 tires over the three days and the only incidents we had were a couple of punctures, including the most unfortunate one with Irvan and the flat-spotted tires on Jimmy Spencer's car." Spencer broke his shoulder in the crash of his McDonald's Ford.

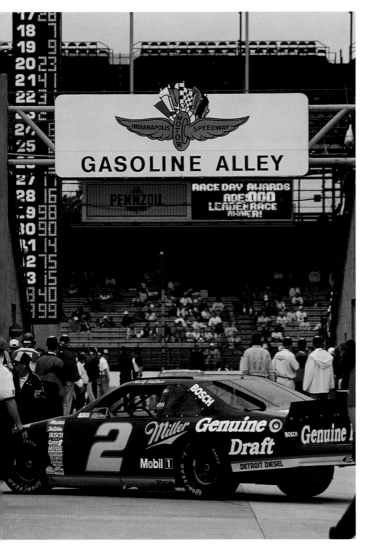

The Brickyard brought a different look to "Gasoline Alley." Stock cars at Indy look, sound, and even smell American. *SCR Archives*

During the national anthem, the pit crews stood in line at their designated pits wearing their team colors. *SCR Archives*

Brickyard Brickbats

Nothing else at the Brickyard measured up to Gordon's Cinderella story. But everyone was a story, particularly feuding brothers Brett and Geoff Bodine, surprise pole-winner Rick Mast, 59-year-old A. J. Foyt, 53-year-old Dave Marcis, the tension of qualifying, and the quirks of the racetrack.

Few will remember that Brett Bodine finished second in the Quaker State Ford, but they'll vividly recall his bumping older sibling Geoff's strong Hoosier-shod Exide Ford out of the race and taking what Geoff called a "family feud" to the track and making it international news. Geoff first tapped Brett on the left rear as he passed, almost causing Brett to lose control. Brett accelerated and bumped Geoff squarely in the rear and into a spin, also taking out Dale Jarrett's Chevrolet in the melee. "He has family problems he's taking out on the track," fumed Geoff Bodine as he climbed out of his wreck. "He's my brother. I love him. But he spun me out." Brett allowed that he had a better line into the turn and bumped his brother accidentally. "I'd never take family problems to the track," says Brett, adding that he hadn't spoken to his brother in more than two months. "It wasn't intentional. I don't race my brothers. I race the cars."

The Rainbow Warriors were quick and intense all race, performing flawlessly stop after stop. Consistent pit stops helped Gordon keep the DuPont Chevrolet up front and into victory circle. *SCR Archives*

NASCAR ruled the incident a racing accident and levied no fines or penalties. "Personal problems are out of our jurisdiction until they become evident on the track," says NASCAR's Kevin Triplett, noting that the sanctioning body was not aware of any personal differences until after the incident. Todd Bodine, the third brother in the race who finished an impressive ninth in the Mock Motorsports/Factory Stores Ford, speculated that his mother would put a quick end to the feud. "Mom's the boss in the family," Todd says. "I wouldn't want to be Brett or Geoff."

The race was manna for the needy. Only three of the top-10 finishers had won a race this season. Brett Bodine is leaving Kenny Bernstein's team for another ride or his own team, gaining him bargaining power. Bill Elliott's third place helped cinch a sponsorship deal for 1995 with McDonald's (Chairman Ed Rensi was watching) as the driver departs Junior Johnson to return to a family operation in Dawsonville, Georgia. Three-time champion Darrell Waltrip, written off by some as a winner, rebuffed critics with a strong sixth. Seventh-place Ken Schrader in the Kodiak Chevrolet enhanced Hendrick Motorsports' windfall performance.

Rusty Wallace had a solid fourth in the Miller Ford at the speedway where team-owner Roger Penske is king of the 500 and the fifth-place performance of Earnhardt and the Goodwrench Chevrolet outfit was vintage championship stuff. Earnhardt started second and twice overcame setbacks to roar to the front. "I

Gordon held the DuPont Chevrolet steady as Ernie Irvan brought the Havoline Ford right up on his rear bumper. On the backstraight with five laps remaining, the two touched lightly coming out of turn two; midway down the straight the right-front tire of Irvan's Ford went flat. Gordon, who had turned 23 years old two days earlier, went on to capture the big "Brick." *SCR Archives*

think I passed more cars than anybody," he says. "I sure wanted to get up there with Jeff and Ernie. "Dale and the whole team were absolutely remarkable," owner Richard Childress says "Next time we'll be better prepared."

Qualifying Jitters

Qualifying was a race in itself and a war of nerves. Among the 83 entries, 69 cars attempted to qualify for the top 20 first-round positions. There were 53 assaults on the final 20 spots. Some drivers, among them H. B. Bailey, more at home on occasional visits to old Darlington Raceway, and James Hylton, attempted to qualify for the experience and memory, though they had no chance of cracking the field. Bailey can always savor that he was officially the first on the track.

Gordon, who qualified third, and Geoff Bodine, who was fourth, set the tone. "I thought my heart was going to come out of my chest I was so excited and nervous," Gordon says. "It is such a relief to make the field."

"I've been racing something for 40 years," says Bodine, "and I have never been so anxious. Indy and this race are one of a kind. We tried to play that aspect down. But believe me, every guy here had butterflies."

Mast's pole-winning speed of 172. 414 miles per hour (52.000 seconds) was a surprise to the estimated pole-day crowd of 100,000, but not to the low-key Skoal Racing Ford team. Foyt, also sponsored by U.S. Tobacco's Copenhagen brand, helped crew chief Kevin Hamlin and owner Richard Jackson fine-tune the new car in tests and offered pole-day tips. "After the thunderstorm three hours before qualifying, we were confused," says Mast, "and worried about what the track would do. We consulted A. J., and he told us the track would be tight, to leave the car alone.

"The track changed as often as a traffic signal. It was real tight when we first got out to practice and it got slicker and slicker as qualifying time approached. Then it rained. . . ."

Mast, a farm boy from rural Rockbridge Baths, Virginia, basked in the brightest limelight of his career, though his bid for his first Winston Cup victory at NASCAR's biggest race was short-circuited by ignition problems. He did get to retell the story of selling a Black Angus beef cow for $575 to finance his first race car, a 1957 Chevrolet. He was nabbed for speeding on the way to his first race and applied

It seems everyone was going for right-side tires and the pits were buzzin' all race long at the fast flat track.

Nigel Kinrade

the $28 in winnings to the traffic ticket. He and Jackson received $50,000 and a luxury van for winning the pole, and he was thrilled to lead the first lap of the race.

"In spite of the outcome, this was a boost to our two-year program to improve on flat tracks," Jackson says. "We've had good cars and runs, but we've fallen out too often with mechanical problems. Rick has proved he's a good driver, but he needs a team behind him to give him a win."

Foyt's Return to Indy

One of the highlights of Dave Marcis' big-league career of 752 starts—qualifying 16th—was ruined when his new Chevrolet was victim of a crash with Mike Chase, the only NASCAR Winston West driver to make the field. The small, independent owner/driver who depends on sponsorship race-by-race, a passing breed in the sport, had failed to qualify for four races this season.

The owner of Terramite Construction Equipment Company, of Charleston, West Virginia, had given Marcis enough money (rumored at $50,000) to finance a first-class Brickyard effort. Marcis was able to afford a new car and all the trimmings. He was invited by Earnhardt and Childress to their three-car test at Indy and applied the data to his car. "This just shows what we can do with enough money and time to prepare for a race," Marcis says. "I was so excited after I qualified [at 169.514] that when Helen [his wife] walked into the garage I shook her hand. It's a shame to get put out in a crash, but I wanted to be a part of this and I was."

Then there was Foyt, whose return to the speedway where he won four 500s and retired from Indy cars in 1992, was applauded by everyone but his wife, Lucy. She was upset with his racing again and told him in no uncertain terms by phone she hoped he didn't qualify. Foyt sweated, swore, and joked until he nailed the 40th and last starting position (except three provisionals) and drove to 30th, four laps down. He could have led a lap during pit stops had the Ford he owns not run out of gas. That is, after "we used a Jaws of Life to get him into the car," joked a friend from Goodyear.

"I didn't say I would retire. I said I wouldn't get back in an Indy car," says Foyt, who received an ovation akin to Gordon's from the fans. "I wanted to come back to Indy for the first NASCAR race, even though I hadn't driven a stock car in about five years, or one on a flat track since Ontario [California] in the late 1970s.

"I can't blame my wife for being upset. She's bandaged me and pushed me around over the years. I don't know if this is my last race. I'm not making predictions. I'll be 60 years old next year and this is a young man's game, like the kid [Gordon], who did a great job. But I really had a lot of fun." Perhaps enough, he hinted, to occasionally bring him back to the circuit.

In addition to Foyt and NASCAR-regular John Andretti, Indy car drivers Geoff Brabham and Danny Sullivan cracked the field in their first Winston Cup race. Brabham crashed out, finishing 38th. Experienced in IROC Series stockers, Brabham qualified an impressive 18th in a Ford, and owners Michael Kranefuss, former director of motorsports at Ford, and Carl Haas, owner of an IndyCar team, indicated that he might drive other selected races for the new NASCAR outfit. And that Kmart might reappear as sponsor. Sullivan, the 1985 500 champion driving a Chevrolet fielded by Indianapolis corporations, went the distance in spite of a spinout and says he is likely to try NASCAR again.

The First Run

The inaugural Brickyard 400 was largely an experiment for drivers and teams. "It felt funny for a six-time champion to be a rookie," says Earnhardt. While chassis requirements were similar to Pocono International Raceway's 2.5-mile triangle, IMS, a 2.5-mile rectangle with four distinct turns connected by short chutes, was a challenge, especially its high sensitivity to heat and changeable conditions.

Evernham closely guarded his setup. "I think our setup was unusual, but that's all I'll say. The speedway is the smoothest and most reactive to temperature that we race on," he says. "When the sun comes out, the surface gets slick and loses its grip. If you have a push, it's aggravated. Balance is essential, or you'll get into a push/loose situation. Our car got looser as the temperature rose during the race, although that was only seven degrees. We were the worst in the last sixty miles. What we tried to do was make a stock car act like an Indy car. We'll be running the new Monte Carlo next year and that will present a different situation."

Adds Ricky Rudd, 11th in the Tide Ford, "We just missed the setup. We started with too little rear spoiler. We got into the draft early and the car was loose. We raised the spoiler. Then we had the wrong gear. We went real tall with the gear, thinking attrition would be high—like Pocono. Raising the spoiler killed two hundred rpm.

"I thought the track would be hard on the valvetrain. Basically, you have two Pocono straights. That's the hardest track on the valvetrain. We turned eighty-eight hundred rpm in practice. We figured that would sling the guts out of the engine in the race. So we were geared wrong. The story is, we wish we could race again tomorrow."

Secure in history and with their winning Lumina, "Booger," headed for the speedway's Hall of Fame Museum, Gordon, Evernham, and the team continue to pursue lofty goals with renewed vigor.

"Winning the Brickyard 400 is just incredible," Gordon says, "but the Winston Cup championship is the topper of them all, the ultimate. That won't happen this year. We are a team of the future. Right now we are learning the ropes and the racetracks. My driving and our team are getting better. After the Brickyard, we needed one more win to achieve our goals this season—three wins, tenth ranking in points, and a pole that put us back in the Busch Clash."

Gordon paused and laughed. "Hey, I'm still a kid at heart. I love to play video games."

GETTING PERSONAL WITH JEFF GORDON

STAFF REPORT
Stock Car Racing, April 1995

Has Success Spoiled the Young Man from Sprint Car Racing?

SCR Archives

The guard was just doing his job. He kept an eye on this young guy with the blue jeans, sneakers, and the dark glasses, and as the suspect walked along the fence encircling the VIP parking area where all the top Winston Cup drivers had set up their custom motor coaches, the guard snapped into full alert. Now the kid came to a gate in the fence, and shoved it open.

"Hey!" the guard yelled. "You can't go in there."

Jeff Gordon, 23, stopped in his tracks. Maybe he has always been someplace where it didn't look like he belonged. He raced sprint cars at age 13, and, Lord, how they had howled about that. He was in a Winston Cup car at 21, earlier than anyone is supposed to be. Now Gordon just wanted to climb into his home away from home and relax for a couple of hours, and, one more time, somebody wasn't quite sure he had any business there.

The guard walked closer. Gordon said nothing. Suddenly, the guard displayed an embarrassed grin.

"Sorry, Jeff," he said. "Didn't recognize you with your sunglasses on."

Gordon waved. "No problem." He walked on, then looked back toward the guard and said, "Thanks for watching."

Hell, there has never been any way *not* to watch Jeff Gordon.

He showed up in big-league stock car racing just in time for the 1992 season-closer at Atlanta. It was straight out of Hollywood: Richard Petty, king, ending his career on the same afternoon when Jeff Gordon, prince, untied the ribbon on his.

Back then, he was a kid who had won in everything he'd ever driven, from quarter midgets to Busch Grand Nationals, and when they asked him about the pressure of moving to Winston Cup—especially with one of the sport's wealthiest car owners, Rick Hendrick, and maybe its richest sponsor, DuPont—Gordon just shrugged and said he'd always been able to handle pressure before.

Now Jeff Gordon, 23, sat at a table in his big blue Newell bus, eating potato chips out of a huge bag and drinking spring water from a plastic bottle. He was, after just two Winston Cup point race wins, already a superstar. No getting around that. He had attained that rank not simply because of what he had done, but because of the ease and grace with which he did it. And, certainly, because of what everyone seems so sure he will do in the future. It is a phenomenon common in sports, but brand new to racing: superstardom on speculation. Yet, despite the hype, you know that Gordon is the genuine article, the real goods.

I asked him about the pressure he had shrugged off in the beginning and how he figured things had gone so far.

"Well, pressure is handled easily by performance," he said, "so we've done all right there. Getting to this level of performance, that was the hard part."

He meant the level that won Charlotte for him last May, and then let him pull off the biggest stock car jewel heist of all time in the Brickyard 400 at Indianapolis. Like he said, it took some time to get there: in 1993, you didn't automatically pencil in Gordon's number 24 as a pre-race pick; today, it is among the favorites on any given Sunday.

"Not too many rookies come into Winston Cup racing with a team like I did," he acknowledged. "That took a lot of the pressure off."

I said, "But looking back, has there been more pressure than you expected there would be?"

"Definitely," Gordon answered. "I never knew what a big change it would be, just jumping over the line from Busch Grand National to Winston Cup. You think you've made it big when you go Busch racing—and it's a great series, don't get me wrong—but when you get to Winston Cup, it's a whole new world. There's so much more media stuff, so many more fans, so many more, um, demands.

"But pressure is just part of racing. I put a lot of pressure on myself. Nobody wants to win any more than me. That pressure pushes aside whatever pressure comes from the outside."

Maybe so, but never had any Winston Cup newcomer faced more outside expectations than Jeff Gordon had. Why, even prior to Gordon's first season, Charlotte Motor Speedway president Humpy Wheeler, a talent scout of considerable repute, had told me, "Jeff is one of those guys who comes along every 25 years or so, like a Foyt or a Petty or an Andretti." He was, depending on what you read, the new Richard Petty, the best prospect since Dale Earnhardt, the most naturally gifted NASCAR arrival since Tim Richmond, or all three.

Gordon smiled and said, "I've always been 'the young kid.' Everybody's always written, you know, 'He's young, he's done this and done that. Now can he do it here?' I try not to read a lot of that stuff."

There's always a request for Jeff Gordon's time. Here, he poses atop an asphalt milling machine for a Dover Downs PR photo.
SCR Archives

When Jeff Gordon was just a kid sprint car racer, life was simpler. But he says he appreciates where he's at, loves it in fact. *SCR Archives*

Think about that for a second: How many kid race drivers do you know, in their teens or early 20s, at any level of the sport, who could truthfully say they don't tear through trade papers looking for any sign of their names? Gordon said he doesn't, and you know what? I believe him. I think he passed that stage a long time ago.

"I know what my job is," Jeff Gordon said. "That's all that really matters. Whatever anybody says or writes isn't important to me."

Gordon's public relations guy is a fellow named Ron Miller. He was a newspaperman, and a good one, before he got out of that racket and set up his own PR agency in Charlotte. We were talking about Gordon's personal appearance schedule, and Miller said he'd get me a copy of a typical month's list of obligations. He got me two months instead. The first month, September, had 16 dates; the second, October, had 17. Neither number included races or time trials or test sessions, just those occasions when Jeff Gordon, 23, gave a speech to sales executives, signed autographs, or taped a TV interview.

His isn't the most cluttered calendar in Winston Cup racing, but it's not exactly a life of leisure, either. Miller attached a yellow Post-It note to the schedules he gave me; it read, "Add in all the impromptu stuff, and he's a pretty busy boy."

I asked Gordon how much he had to do with the planning of his own schedule. He said, "The way it goes, usually, is that seventy percent of it goes through Ron's office. Maybe another twenty percent goes to my stepdad, John Bickford. The other ten percent comes to me.

"Most of the stuff we do involves DuPont or Valvoline or Kellogg's or McDonald's, people who are direct sponsors. Each sponsor has a certain number of appearances they get; the associate sponsors get a certain amount too. Add all of those up, plus the races and the test days, and there's not a whole lot left."

The "impromptu stuff" Ron Miller referred to happens at the racetrack. There are always writers who need a quote for tomorrow's edition, TV people who want a sound bite, and fans dying to get their souvenir programs signed. It is life in the Winston Cup garage area, an interview here, a pack of autograph hounds there, and, before you know it, the hour-long break between practice and qualifying is gone.

This increased tugging and pulling—smothering might be a more accurate description—has shortened the tempers of more than a few drivers, car owners, and crew chiefs lately.

"You've got to learn how to deal with that stuff," Gordon said, "because if you let it get to you, your focus is not on what you're there to do. You have to focus on the racing. Do all that other stuff too—the autographs and the interviews—and have a good attitude about it. But focus on the racing, and it will work out right."

I said, "How much has the demand for your time changed since the Brickyard win?"

"I would say it's probably doubled," Gordon said. "I don't see all of the requests for interviews and appearances, but I know they've definitely increased. And I know that around the racetracks, things have changed. It seems like I've been signing things nonstop ever since we won that race.

"I had never signed pit passes before, but I've signed so many from Indianapolis. I've signed 'em for other crew members, NASCAR inspectors, you name it."

He said he has been able to measure his rising fame in another way too. "You have to have somebody take you in and out of the racetrack, so you can kinda hide in the back and sneak past everybody."

Gordon frowned. "It's not necessarily that you *want* to hide, but sometimes you *have* to."

Here is why: because you can never give some fans enough. A Winston Cup fan might say he just wants to catch a glimpse of his favorite driver, but if the driver acknowledges that glimpse, there is often an attempt at conversation; if the driver stops long enough to chat, somebody wants an autograph; if the driver signs one autograph, he'd better be ready to sign a hundred or more, on the spot. It is a game the driver cannot win, so most drivers, especially after a race, when they're physically and emotionally drained, choose not to even play. They just try to get away as quickly and quietly as possible.

Following the race at North Wilkesboro last fall, Gordon was stuck in traffic trying to get out of the infield. He was riding in the back of a van driven by Rick Dameron, who works for Ron Miller. The van had small DuPont logos on it, and before long it was surrounded by race-goers anxious to (a) figure out if Jeff Gordon was in there, and (b) get a look at him if indeed he was. Some of the more, uh, rabid fans actually climbed up the small aluminum ladder mounted on the truck's rear doors, trying to peek through the windows.

Gordon appreciates his fans even though their demands can be occasionally oppressive.
SCR Archives

You think race drivers aren't in demand?

Something else to ponder: You think everyone could handle that?

We talked some more about his schedule, and Jeff Gordon said that what nobody stops to consider is that, after all the racing and testing and appearances are done, "You've still got a life. You've still got Christmas and Thanksgiving and the rest. You've still got a family. You've still got certain things you have to take care of."

He laughed. "You've still got to do your laundry, answer your mail."

"How many hours in an average day," I said, "are actually yours alone, or yours and [your wife] Brooke's, when there are no outside intrusions on your time?"

Jeff Gordon, 23, sighed. "We have to *make* days. We literally have to schedule days to ourselves. And even when I do have a day to myself, in the back of my mind I'm always thinking, 'Gosh, I hope I wasn't supposed to call anybody today,' or 'Was I supposed to sign something for somebody?'

"If I didn't stop and say, 'Hey, I've got to take this particular day off,' there wouldn't *be* any days off."

He said, quite earnestly, "Thank goodness for Ron [Miller] and his people. They're the ones who have to answer all the phone calls, and have to turn down a lot of things because the schedule is just too full. And because they know I want to keep my sanity."

I asked Gordon a question that everyone who attains a certain degree of fame must deal with sooner or later: "Does it ever get tough to figure out who's a real friend, and who's there just because of who you are and what you've done?"

He took a few moments to answer.

Gordon will tell you how important his stepfather, John Bickford, has been in the development of his career. *SCR Archives*

"Sometimes it's hard, yeah," he said finally. "I mean, I'm no Michael Jordan. I'm no Dale Earnhardt, either. But, yeah, I do see what you're talking about. It's not at a level that I think is a problem, or anything like that. But there's times when you wonder who your friends really are. There are people who'll try to be your friend so they can get closer to you, for whatever reason. I try not to let that happen.

"I have very few close friends," he said, sounding more candid than sad. "My closest friend is Brooke because she's basically the same age I am, and we like the same things, and we do everything together.

"It's hard for me to have a lot of friends. You have to understand, I work on the weekends, and most other people my age work during the week. When they're hanging out, I'm working. When I'm hanging out, they're working. It's tough just to have fun with the friends I do have, and to go and do the things that normal 23-year-olds do. That's why Brooke and I spend so much of our time together. We go to the movies, get out on the Sea-Doos. We do things ourselves.

"I try not to get too close to anybody who's directly involved in racing. Sure, I try to be friendly with everybody, but, you know, racing has turned into a business. As much fun as it is, and as much as I enjoy it, there's times when business decisions need to be made. And when you've got friends involved, it makes those decisions even tougher."

Gordon chuckled. "As far as having friends on the racetrack," he said, "that's tough. I don't want to not race a guy hard for the win because he's my buddy. And if you run into somebody and he's your friend, what happens then? Are you not friends anymore? You need to have a good understanding of where all of that ends."

He said that all his life, most of his friends have been older guys, mechanics and racers and fans in a half-dozen different forms of racing.

"I think having friends who were older than me helped me mature a little bit quicker. It helped me grow up.

"I'm still a kid—I like video games and neat cars and that kind of junk—but ever since I can remember, I was hanging out with people who were four, five, six years older than I was. Even now, almost everybody seems to be older than me."

I said, "Is it possible for you to go out for dinner, especially on a race weekend, and really enjoy a meal without people stopping by the table to chat?"

He laughed. "It's funny you'd ask that. I was very surprised by something that happened just last night. I went right down the street here, to a place I figured was going to be packed with race fans. I was kinda hesitant when we pulled in because the parking lot was full. But I was starving, and there wasn't really anyplace else to go.

"So we went in there," Gordon said, "and there wasn't one person who said anything to me about racing."

But that, Gordon admitted, was a rarity.

"Usually, anytime you're out someplace where there's a race, you run into people. You have to be careful because you don't want to put yourself into a position where you might…"

He paused.

"…uh, cause a bad situation."

I asked him what he meant.

"Well," Gordon said, "you're trying to eat, or get to the rest room, and…"

He paused again. It was as if he knew what he wanted to say, but didn't know quite how to say it without sounding, well, like one more celebrity whining about being a celebrity.

Finally, he said, "If you go somewhere where you know there are going to be race fans, you shouldn't go there thinking you want peace and quiet. It's not going to happen. You shouldn't expect it to happen. If you want to get away where you can enjoy a nice dinner, you've got to use some common sense, and go someplace you know is quiet.

"If you go into a place where there's a lot of race fans, you can almost guarantee that somebody's going to come over to see you. And you can't be rude to those people, or mean to 'em, or push 'em away. That's not the right thing to do.

"So you have control over what happens. It's your choice. You just have to use common sense."

I suggested that it is a lesser-of-two-evils problem: If you accommodate the fan, it takes away from your own evening out, and you suffer a little bit; but if you don't accommodate him, he sees you forever in a bad light, and you suffer forever.

Gordon shrugged, and said, "Exactly."

Then he added, "But I also know that I'm not always going to make everybody happy. There might be some people who see me on a bad day, and it will change their outlook on me. There's nothing I can do about that.

"I try to give people the same respect they give me. If I'm eating in a restaurant, and somebody waits until I'm not busy or not eating before they come over, then it's no problem. I'll talk to 'em, sign something for 'em, whatever they want. It's like, OK, they showed you a little respect, now you should show them the respect of giving them what they want."

Gordon came up the hard way, racing sprint cars and midgets. Here, he's behind the wheel of a midget on the big Phoenix mile. He doesn't race cars like this anymore, but he makes a whole lot more money than when he did. *SCR Archives*

We talked a bit about how being pestered in restaurants goes with the territory, how it is part of the price you pay for being successful in a public occupation. I wondered if maybe there were times, like on those bad days he mentioned, when the price seemed too high.

Gordon kicked that one around, and then said, "Well, maybe it is a high price. But I think you've got to add up all the plusses and the minuses. And in the long run, believe me, the plusses far outweigh the minuses."

He grinned. "When I sit down and think of all the plusses...

"I mean, I get to drive race cars for a living. I make

Jeff admits that after his Brickyard 400 win he has to make time in his schedule to spend with his new wife Brooke. *SCR Archives*

far more money than I ever thought I could make. I've got fans who'll buy things with my name and my picture on 'em, and cheer me on every weekend. That can't be a bad thing. I can think of a whole lot of other things that would be worse. So, to me, the plusses of being successful are greater than the minuses."

The grin faded now, Jeff Gordon added, "At the same time, my success has made me look at professional athletes and entertainers from a different perspective. I've got a whole new respect for those people. I hear sometimes about an athlete or an actor being rude to somebody, and I always think twice about it. I know what level *I'm* at; I see a Joe Montana or a Bruce Willis, and I can't even begin to imagine what it must be like at their level."

When you talk about fame's upsides and downsides with Jeff Gordon, sooner or later you get around to the mess he refers to as "that Haubstadt deal," Haubstadt being the Indiana town where a quarter-mile dirt track called Tri-County Speedway is located. Gordon, who grew up in Indiana, raced sprinters at Tri-County as a teenager and was supposed to make an appearance there on Saturday, August 7, 1994, the day after the inaugural Brickyard 400 at Indianapolis. "From the Brickyard to the Backyard" was how the track billed it.

At the time he signed the deal, of course, there was no way to know that he would go on to win the historic 400. And there was no way to know that, as a result of that victory, he would be obliged to spend the next day taking part in a NASCAR-orchestrated celebration at Disney World. After all, everybody wants to win, but who in the world actually *plans* to win?

You probably know what happened next: On the afternoon when a few thousand fans converged on tiny little Haubstadt, their hero, Jeff Gordon, winner of the first stock car race ever held at the Indianapolis Motor Speedway, was riding alongside Mickey Mouse in a theme-park parade a thousand miles away. Suffice it to say that the disposition of many a Tri-County spectator did not exactly match the weather in Orlando, which was sunny.

The whole thing turned into a giant public relations headache providing endless fodder for the letters-to-the-editor pages in the trade papers. Folks who had traveled from far and wide to Tri-County Speedway, hoping to see, meet, and chat with Jeff Gordon, blasted him to bits for not showing up.

I asked him if the Haubstadt backlash represented the low point in his relationship with America's race fans. Gordon said simply, "Yeah."

He was quiet for a few seconds. Then, quite firmly, he said, "A lot of people don't realize that NASCAR helped set the whole Disney World thing up. It was very important to NASCAR, and to auto racing in general, to have somebody go to Disney World, just like people from other sports do. That was a big deal.

"I feel like I made the right decision. I mean, who would have been mad if I *hadn't* gone to Disney World? NASCAR would have been upset, and I would have been upset with myself. It wasn't a pleasure trip; I did a lot of business, a lot of satellite interviews from television networks, things like that. It was good for racing.

"I don't like to cancel *anything*. That's just the way I am. But the fact that we won the Brickyard made that Haubstadt deal explode into a big thing."

Some weeks later, Gordon did visit Tri-County, an admitted attempt to smooth the feathers his August 7 no-show had ruffled.

"I think we got things worked out," Gordon said. "We had a great appearance there. I think the fans were happy, and I'm sorry that some of the people who were there the first time didn't get to make it back. But I hope they realize what my situation was."

Not all of them did. Some proclaimed, in this paper or that paper, that Gordon had forgotten where he came from, that he had changed. Gordon said that the angry letters didn't bother him—"That's why I don't read the papers too much"—but he did take offense at the suggestion that his roots now mean nothing to him.

"Nobody knows," Gordon said, frowning, "how much I do remember where I came from. There have been a lot of people who helped get me where I am. Those people who truly helped me get here, they know how much that means to me. They know I haven't forgotten them."

As far as the notion that Jeff Gordon has changed, well, look at it this way: Whose life *isn't* changing at 21, 22, 23?

"No matter what you do, things change," Gordon said. "You can't keep them from changing. You can still be the same person you were ten years ago, but there are things in your life that change. I don't care who you are; when you have a certain amount of success, things have to change. Your privacy level changes, and you change.

"I don't think your judgments or your values change, but you've got to make decisions sometimes that are very difficult and aren't going to make everybody happy. And you've got to be able to live with that.

"I think maybe some people see me and say, 'Here's a guy who's got the world in his hand. He's got everything, and he's just riding along.' It's not like that at all. It hasn't all been easy. It's been a difficult at times, frustrating at times, stressful at times.

"But I have no complaints. I have great parents who gave me the opportunity to be a race car driver. To see the way it's all worked out, it makes my parents heroes in my mind. In Brooke, I met a person who has been wonderful for me. All of that stuff, on top of the racing, is wonderful. I'm so happy with my life right now. I'd be crazy to say I wasn't."

Gordon shook his head, as if this idea was just sinking in for the very first time.

"I live a great life," he said. "I enjoy what I do, and my income is a little bit higher than the average twenty-three-year-old's."

He gestured around the inside of the big motor coach. "I get to have things like *this*."

The shadows are long and Gordon's car isn't all that fast. But when the sun went down, it got much quicker. Crew chief Evernham's masterful call to take only 2 tires with 18 laps to go put Gordon in second and in position to win. *SCR Archives*

He is a kid in a grown-up's world, a boy in a man's game. Yet, somehow, he handles it.

Gordon took a long pull from his bottle of water, and then he laughed out loud.

"When I look back on my life someday," he said, "it's all going to look like a big blur."

It will look that way to everyone else too.

In the end, what sticks with you about Jeff Gordon, is not how old he is, but rather how old he is not. In other words, you look at how much time he has left. Many of his Winston Cup rivals were driving race cars before he was born. One by one—King Richard in 1992, Harry Gant last year—they are driving off into the sunset of retirement. How much longer is Darrell Waltrip going to stick around? Morgan Shepherd? Dick Trickle?

And Jeff Gordon? Well, he turns 40 on August 4, 2011, at which time we will all start looking for the tell-tale signs of age.

One day, I rode with Gordon to an autograph session at City Chevrolet, Rick Hendrick's cornerstone dealership in Charlotte. He drew a crowd estimated by the dealership's management at something between 700 and 800 people. He sat at a table just outside the showroom window, scrawling his name again and again and posing for the occasional Polaroid with somebody's sweetheart.

Among the more unique items Jeff signed that day was a dented and thus discarded right-side door from one of his DuPont Chevrolets. It had somehow found its way into the hands of a fan who was willing to stand in line for hours to have it personalized.

I looked at Gordon sitting there, just a kid, a really good kid, his future as broad as the sky. I wondered what that autographed door might be worth in five or ten years. And I wondered what it might be worth, say, in the year 2011.

FIRST CHAMPIONSHIP: THE JEFF GORDON INTERVIEW

BY FRANK MORIARTY
Circle Track, April 1996

Editor's note: Jeff Gordon won the most Winston Cup races (7) and beat multi-champ Dale Earnhardt for his first Cup title in 1995 by only 34 points – essentially the bonus points he gained by leading the most laps of some races. Not much, but enough. This interview was done shortly afterward and chronicles how he was coping with the demands of his first championship and preparing for future ones.

Being a modern-day Winston Cup champion entails responsibilities such as your appearance on David Letterman's TV show. Could you ever have imagined that these activities would be all in the line of duty for a racer?

I would never have dreamed that. I had no clue that racing would ever lead me to what it has and the opportunities and the things that I do now. It's amazing. I never thought that people would

A relaxed Jeff Gordon is interviewed by MRN radio just before the start of the NAPA 500 and his winning of the 1995 Winston Cup Championship. He qualified eighth for this race and finished 32rd. *SCR Archives*

stand in line to get an autograph from me. I never had any idea that racing would lead to this, that it would be my career and the thing that I do for the rest of my life.

Not only do you have opportunities related to sponsorship commitments, but you've also worked with the Leukemia Society and Cure 2000. How does that tie in with what you have accomplished?

That's part of being successful, sharing with others. Ray Evernham has played a big role in that because of Ray J. [Ray Evernham's young son]. His being diagnosed with leukemia has opened my eyes and a lot of people's eyes to charities and especially the Leukemia Society. When things are going well for you and couldn't be going much better, then you realize that there are other people out there that aren't so fortunate. And children especially, they are the future, our future of America—maybe they aren't getting those opportunities that you're getting. You can show other people out there that if you contribute you can save lives today. It means a lot to me, and I hope I can help get the word out to others. By myself, I cannot contribute enough money—even as much money as I make, if I contributed everything it wouldn't be enough to make a difference. So that's why I like to try to do as much as I can, but also get the word out to as many other people also.

Has winning the championship sunk in now in the wake of the Winston Cup banquet in New York? How long does it take for the realization to come that something you've worked so hard for has finally been accomplished?

It's certainly sinking in. I don't know when it stops sinking in! Last night I was in Atlanta and did an appearance. It was really the first autograph session I did since I won the championship, and I noticed a big difference. There were a lot more people there than usual, and they all were shouting, "Hey champion!" That was quite an experience, quite a thrill, and something that's a part of being the Winston Cup champion.

Championship Difference

How does winning the championship differ from winning something like the Brickyard 400?

Well, I think you can go out there, and you can have a good day. You can hit it right on one day, and we feel like that was our day at the Brickyard. It was like it was meant to be, like a fantasy that came true because we wanted it so bad. But to win a championship you've got to do it throughout the whole year. You can't just hit it every once in a while, you've got to hit it all the time and have the consistency—you can't fall out of races. After last year and the year before, I realized how difficult it is to win a championship. We're all the time trying to finish every race, finish as far forward as possible, knowing that the best we've done is eighth in points. To go out there and have a year like we did this

Above: Gordon and his young team had to withstand a furious end of the year run by Dale Earnhardt and his veteran squad to win their first Cup championship. They didn't crack. *SCR Archives*

Left: Ray Evernham's learned his craft as a modified driver/mechanic; he was essentially unknown at the Cup level when Rick Hendrick agreed to pair him with Gordon. *SCR Archives*

year is amazing. I think other people look at it the same way. They think, "OK, it's one thing for him to win races, but to be a champion, now that's something!" If you look back at how many people have won championships, you see it's pretty hard to come by. Only the guys that have been the best have gone on to win championships.

There was a bit of controversy when you left Bill Davis and the Ford program to enter Winston Cup by going with Rick Hendrick and Chevrolet for 1993. How do you look back on that now? Have all the fences been mended from that period of time?

They certainly haven't been mended because Bill Davis and I don't have the relationship that we used to have. We got along real well, liked working together, but that whole situation happened because I was forced to make a decision. I wanted to go Winston Cup racing the next year; I felt like that was the year for me to move on. I was needing to make a decision right then because I had some offers coming in to me. But I wanted to stick with Bill Davis. He had helped me get a good start in Busch Grand National, and Ford Motor Company had helped me out.

I had Ford Motor Company telling me, "Hey, we'll put you in a Ford whether it's Bill Davis or somebody else." And I said, "Well, who are you going to put me with?" They mentioned some teams, and they weren't teams that I felt were winning, and they weren't teams that I felt were going to really improve and be something that was a good move for Jeff Gordon. Then, with the Bill Davis situation, we were just waiting to get a sponsorship.

It's tough when you're somebody that has no experience as a driver, who's only 20 or 21 years old, and you have no experience as a car owner. We weren't really getting any leads, we weren't getting any positive things to talk about. It just didn't seem like the sponsors were coming. I'd already been talked to by a couple of other Winston Cup owners. One of them was real positive, but when Rick Hendrick came along it just happened to be the right time. We were running out of time with Bill Davis, and it was a great opportunity that would have been difficult for me to turn down. Now I can say that I made the right decision, and nobody can argue with me. But back then, it was the hardest thing I've ever had to do.

Jeff Gordon's crew keeps him up front in the July 1995 Pepsi 400. Dale Earnhardt started on the pole and Gordon third, but the youngster beat the big-track master for the win in that championship season. *SCR Archives*

Gordon and Evernham celebrate their first win at New Hampshire in 1995, after starting 21st. *SCR Archives*

Why Gordon (here in BGN sponsor Baby Ruth colors) wasn't locked under contract when driving for Ford is an all-time motorsports snafu. Young racers weren't supposed to win right out of the box, so why tie up capital in a contract? Gordon forever changed that thinking. *SCR Archives*

Toward the end of your first full season of Busch racing, I asked you what it was going to be like moving into Winston Cup. Your answer was, "I'm pretty sure it's going to take a whole year or two to learn those cars." But really, you were competitive almost immediately. Why do you think you found success so quickly?

Probably because of Rick Hendrick's resources, and also because Ray Evernham went with me. I think that's been the key to a lot of the success. If you look at when I was winning races in Busch Grand National, Ray was there, and since I've been in Winston Cup, Ray has been there. He and I just really work well together. And I think that not many rookies can come into Winston Cup and have the type of cars, equipment, resources, and people that I've been able to have at Hendrick's.

In 1993, you won one of the Twin 125s and also had 11 top 10s in the rest of that year. You mentioned the resources of Hendrick Motorsports, but did it surprise you to run that strongly right off the bat?

Yes, especially at Daytona—I haven't won a Twin 125 since. That was definitely something that was really surprising. You never really know how things are going to go, but I think that first year got me excited for the next year and probably led to the championship coming so early in our third year. When we found out how good we were going to run in our first year, we thought, "This is going to be great. We're going to get some experience, learn from these things, and hopefully great things are going to happen."

Stepping Up

Well, that is what did happen. In 1994 you won the Busch Clash, the 600 in Charlotte, and then the Brickyard 400. Did you feel that stepping up your program to that level was a logical step based on the performance that you laid down in 1993?

Definitely. We were trying to win a race that first year, and we came close and had a second a couple of times. The next step was to win a race. You make that your goal, and you think you can do it, but when it actually happens at this level it's amazing. That's why our emotions really showed when we won the Coca-Cola 600. And I don't think we could have gone and won the Brickyard if we hadn't first won the Coca-Cola 600. That was real exciting to win not just one race, but two of the biggest races on the circuit in our second year.

Did you feel any pressure during the 1995 season to focus more on consistency rather than aggressiveness, and how do you set a balance? Do you put the points race out of your mind? That must be easier said than done . . .

Yes, but you definitely try to not think about the championship. Because really, you want to go out there and win every race if it's possible—you want to try to at least do that. I think that's what we did. We went out there and just tried to go to the front, tried to lead laps, and tried to win races. When we look back now, our bonus points from leading laps certainly paid off. I think that was a major contributor to the championship, and I think because we went out there trying to win and not just trying to finish we bettered our finishes. But at the same time, when you do that you sometimes put yourself in a bad position, situations where you take extra chances can cause you either problems or cause you to make mistakes on the racetrack. So it was one of those deals where we were aggressive, we were trying to win races, and when we realized that we had a shot at winning the championship, that's when we started to try to build the consistency a little more and had 14 top 10s in a row.

What can you tell me about Ray Evernham, not only as far as race day but how he directs your race team during the week?

Ray is a lot like a coach; he's a great motivator, and he's a good friend of mine. I don't think our team could be as successful without him. He's been in a race car before and knows how to relate to what I'm

Weekly races telecast on ESPN helped propel a teenage Jeff Gordon to stardom. *SCR Archives*

saying. He's just the perfect kind of crew chief for me, and not every crew chief would be able to work with me. Because I'm the type of driver where I know what I feel and just relate back to the crew chief what I'm feeling, and what I need in the car instead of knowing that if I'm feeling this, I need this, this, and this in the car. I don't have that much experience yet, so Ray and I really just complement each other.

In 1996 Ray is going to have increased responsibilities as team manager with both the No. 24 and the No. 25 car. Are you at all concerned about this and have you talked with Ray about it?

I've certainly talked to Ray about it, and it's definitely not a concern—I think it's something that's going to help us. Ray wouldn't have done it if he didn't think it would help out both teams, and I don't think I would have agreed with it if I thought it was going to hurt us. I think it's only going to make my team, Kenny's team, and all the Hendrick Motorsports teams even stronger.

> *"When he'd call me 'Wonder Boy' and things like that, I stuck to my own thing and didn't really mess around."*
>
> —Jeff Gordon on Dale Earnhardt

Earnhardt Intimidation?

What was it like racing Dale Earnhardt for the championship? He is reputed to be a master at intimidating people he races by just kind of hanging around you and always making his presence felt. Were you aware of any extra attention Dale was directing your way?

No, not really. I thought it was a real privilege to be able to race with Dale, and I respect him a whole lot. He'd jab at me every once in a while trying to get me to loosen up and have fun, and I think he saw how focused I was and that I didn't really get into the fun. When he'd call me "Wonder Boy" and things like that, I stuck to my own thing and didn't really mess around. But I had a great time this year. I didn't really see Dale being "The Intimidator" off the racetrack, but he's always carrying that on the racetrack. Any time you're around him, if he's running good he's going to be tough to beat. . . . It seemed like this year when he was running good I wasn't, and when I was running good he wasn't running as good—so we never really had any hard, tight battles other than a couple of times.

Dale seems to be good with his ways of using the media to get his messages across. For example, you mentioned the "Wonder Boy" nickname, and he's also said he's the first man to win the Brickyard 400. Saying things to your face is one thing, but does it bother you when he resorts to using a forum where millions of people will hear what he says?

I was watching Jay Leno when Dale was on, and I just laughed about it. Because I know Dale, and I know he's just having fun. It's no more than just his way of having a good time. He's been racing a long, long time and there's no reason to be so serious all the time. So I laugh at it. That's why, when I went to the banquet, I'd been serious all year long, so I thought, "Now I'm going to have a little fun with it."

Of course, immediately after Atlanta, he was still saying the same kind of things. Do you look at that as just Dale trying to lay a little groundwork for 1996?

Oh, I'm sure. He showed he was very, very strong at Atlanta, but we all get to work all winter and get prepared for Daytona and start all over again.

Speaking of Daytona and starting all over again, with so many demands and distractions that come with being the Winston Cup champion, have you thought about what you need to do to maintain your competitive focus so you can hopefully repeat next season?

I think organizing my schedule is going to be the most important thing, so that I'm not too strung out and doing too many things. Really, I've never had a problem with that in the past. When you get in the race car, you shut off all those outside things and all you think about and all you focus on is that race car. Hopefully, we'll be able to do it again this year.

Your first Winston Cup start was at Atlanta in Richard Petty's last race. Three years later you win the championship at that same track. A lot of people are saying that this symbolizes a new era in NASCAR with an influx of talented, young drivers like yourself, Bobby Labonte, Ward Burton, and others. Do you personally feel a part of a new wave in Winston Cup racing?

Well, yes. I think there's always going to be new people coming along and younger guys coming along—that's what keeps the sport going. I think right now is a great time. There's a lot of talented young guys that are getting in some good race cars, and I'm just one of many.

Just for a moment, think of these names: Richard Petty, Bobby Isaac, Ned Jarrett, David Pearson, Cale Yarborough. They are all legendary NASCAR champions, and now your name is right alongside of theirs. How does that make you feel?

Gordon contributes his valuable time to charitable causes.
SCR Archives

Oh, I know how special it is to be Winston Cup champion. It's something that I'll be able to remember and enjoy for the rest of my life because every time they introduce me it's going to be as the 1995 Winston Cup champion. That's a great feeling. It's a great accomplishment and I'm very proud to be a part of it. I'm glad that my team could be a part of it. I'm just looking forward to all of the great things that are going to happen in the future from this championship. One thing about great champions in Winston Cup is that the truly great champions are the ones who have won more than one championship. That's something that is very, very hard to do. I'm very proud to be able to say that I've won one and it's quite an accomplishment, but to be able to say I've won more than one is something even greater. That's why when you go to New York, and you enjoy New York as much as you can, that's an incentive to come back and do it all again.

JEFF GORDON'S PROBLEM

In 1995 he outran Earnhardt, won the Winston Cup title, and stepped onto center stage. Now comes the hard part.

STAFF REPORT
Stock Car Racing, March 1996

Jeff Gordon puts some body English into the game now, his shoulders rising and falling and his hands slapping up against the sides of the pinball machine. *Bang!* He catches the flipper button just right, sends the silver ball smashing into a target, and smiles at the bells and the flashing lights. Gordon has the first Winston Cup championship of his life in his pocket, but to look at him right now you'd think that stock car racing was a million miles away. Only it never is.

The name on the side of the game says "Dr. Dude." The machine once sat in Gordon's basement. Now it rests in a loft in his Hendrick Motorsports race shop, overlooking his team's battalion of Chevrolets, and the same hands that steered those cars to seven wins and $4.4 million in NASCAR prize money in 1995 work only to get Gordon a free ball, an extra shot at Dr. Dude.

And why not? He has earned it. It is a cold, rainy Charlotte afternoon, a day made for "sitting at home and doing absolutely nothing," which Gordon says is his favorite way to spend time off. But doing nothing is not an option for the hottest young race driver in America. Already today, there has been a marathon Goodyear photo shoot at the Hendrick compound. One photographer, one art director, and three assistants dressed Gordon in a rented tuxedo, leaned him on a polished fender, and for the better part of an hour coached him through a crash course in male modeling.

Gordon celebrates his first win at Darlington in 1995. He has six wins there, including three in a row.
SCR Archives

"Smile . . . good, good . . . *click!* . . . now fold your arms . . . *click!* . . . that's it . . . clasp your hands together, just like this . . . good . . . *click!* . . . smile . . . *click!* . . . cross your feet . . . *click!* . . . good, good . . . *click!*"

Now he is back in his boy-next-door clothes, jeans and sneakers and a pullover shirt, relaxing with his pinball game. Dr. Dude makes some more noise, and a message—"You're a major dude"—scrolls across the screen in front of him. Jeff Gordon laughs.

I ask him a question few 24-year-old champions ever hear: "Have you ever thought about how much longer you'd like to race?"

For all the mind games that Earnhardt played with Gordon and other racers, he respected one of the few racers that could beat him and offered advice when asked. *SCR Archives*

It produces a lengthy pause. "Well, I haven't thought about that a lot," Gordon says. "But I want to race as long as I'm competitive, and as long as I like what I'm doing. Which is kind of the same thing, because when I'm not competitive, I won't be having a good time. Someday there's going to be some new young drivers coming up, wearing me out, and I'll just decide to retire."

I mention that I only asked because right now, with NASCAR's public appeal at an all-time high, he and Dale Earnhardt clearly stand together as the sport's marquee stars. For 1995, anyway, they had center stage to themselves, and everyone else was sort of off in the wings. And center stage comes with a price; there are a million appearances to make, demands from sponsors, hordes of autograph seekers inside every race-town restaurant, and media people who always want more. Some great drivers have made brief appearances at center stage and never returned, almost as if the spotlight has driven them off. Only Earnhardt, who at 44 has been at center stage for roughly 10 years, since winning the second of his seven Winston Cup titles in 1986, has stood the test of time.

"As young as you are," I tell Jeff Gordon, "you might be in for another twenty years of this stuff."

He grins. "Good problem to have, huh?"

But his grin is only temporary. Gordon asks me to think about what he has just said. "It's good," he explains, "but it's still a problem."

Gordon sought out seasoned veterans like Mark Martin for advice at Cup tracks to perfect his driving, like he does here at Dover in 1995. He won three straight at the track in 1995 and 1996, and he and Martin share four total wins there. *SCR Archives*

He sighs. "The on-track stuff, the pressure of having to perform out there, is not a problem. The competition is what I like; it keeps you pumped up, keeps you focused. It's the things *off* the racetrack that are harder."

For much of his life, the on-track stuff was all Gordon saw. His early career was put together almost by the numbers, owing to his prodigious talent and the backing of his parents, John and Carol Bickford. It went as trouble-free as could possibly be hoped for. Through every phase to this point—racing sprinters on midwestern dirt tracks at age 14, dominating a televised USAC series in 1989–1990, tackling stock cars as a NASCAR Busch Series driver in 1991, and then capturing top Winston Cup rookie honors in 1993—he was seen as a kid, and therefore handled with kid gloves. That all changes now. The pressure from here on will make everything he felt before seem, quite literally, like kid stuff. And Gordon is aware of this.

"I know that over the next few years," he says, "there's going to be a big demand for my time. That's just part of the sport growing, and if you want it to grow, you've got to deal with that."

I say, "So on your bad days—days when you'd like to relax, but instead you've got photo shoots and all this stuff—you never stop and think, Man, not another fifteen years of this . . . ?"

Gordon shakes his head. "If you want to be successful, your private life is gone and your personal time is gone. I knew that going in, so I can't complain about it. My life is good. I can't complain about *any-thing*. What's so bad about this?"

Ray Evernham inspects the damage done to Jeff Gordon's Chevrolet after Gordon wrecked, due to rain, in turns three and four during qualifying at Michigan Speedway in August 1995. *SCR Archives*

Almost in a whisper, Gordon says, "Seven wins. Eight poles. The points. Winning the Winston [Select] at Charlotte. It was just an unbelievable year. Incredible."

"Ever think a championship would come so soon?"

"No," he says. "No, I sure didn't."

Gordon claims that he and crew chief Ray Evernham have been as surprised as anyone by the quantum leaps their team has made.

"In 1993, our rookie year, we ran good," Gordon says. "We came close to winning, and that got us hungry. It gave us the confidence to think, OK, maybe we can win. A little bit into 1994, we won our first race, at Charlotte. It gave us more confidence. Then we won the big one, the Brickyard 400, and we were sure we had learned how to win. What we had to do then was figure out how to run up front consistently, especially in the second half of a season, when it gets physically and mentally tough on everybody. We worked hard on that at the end of 1994, and that brought us into 1995 really pumped up. We felt good about ourselves and our race cars and our engines. Still, we had no idea that 1995 would go like it did."

Last season was a Gordon tour de force, spiked by virtuoso performances in the Winston Select, the July 400 at Daytona, and the Southern 500 at Darlington on Labor Day weekend. In the Select, only Earnhardt and Darrell Waltrip loomed as challengers to Gordon in the final 10-lap shootout, but in their haste to sprint away from him, they crashed. In the summer heat at Daytona, Gordon outran his two premier championship foes at the time, Earnhardt and Sterling Marlin, in a last-lap sprint for the checkers. And after the storied Southern 500 he was ecstatic because, he says, "everybody knows it takes a good driver to win at Darlington."

As interesting as Gordon's other 1995 wins—at Rockingham, Atlanta, Bristol, New Hampshire, and Dover—were the races he could have won. He was a rocket in the Daytona 500 before a botched pit stop; had a dominant ride at Darlington in March only to tangle with slower cars; and was a shoo-in at Pocono in June until he missed a shift and hurt his engine on a critical late restart. He says, "If, and, but, coulda, shoulda, woulda; I don't believe in all that stuff."

His biggest regret about 1995 has nothing to do with lost races, but rather with a lost opportunity. "I've heard Earnhardt say he wishes we could have raced together a little more during the year," Gordon says. "Well, I wish the same thing. Because, I'll tell you, there isn't a better feeling in the world than to race Dale for a win. He is the toughest guy to beat. There isn't anybody who runs harder, or gets more out of a car when he needs to, than Dale. But when we were good [in 1995], he wasn't. When he was good, we weren't."

He skips a beat, and adds this: "The top of the peak."

It is a little bit cocky, sure, but so what? Go beat Earnhardt for the Winston Cup championship, and see if you don't get a little bit cocky yourself.

I ask him how he has changed as a driver, and Gordon says, "The biggest thing is, I've learned to be a lot more patient."

"How so?"

"I saw an interview with [Miami Dolphins quarterback] Dan Marino the other day," he says. "He talked about how he used to get on the other players, and scream and yell a lot. He said it was never because he was angry, but because he wanted perfection. He wanted to win. Well, that's how I am. I have that competitive edge.

"The biggest criticism I've had about this team in the past—and probably the biggest one Ray [Evernham] has had too—is that when things have gone wrong during a race, we've had trouble coming back. I blame myself for a lot of that because sometimes I'd get frustrated. I'd never give up, but I'd be frustrated. Unfortunately, my frustration always came out on the radio. It took me a while to realize that screaming and yelling on the radio doesn't do me any good, and it certainly doesn't do my guys any good. If I'm screaming and yelling, they're not going to be very happy.

"So in 1995," Gordon says, "I tried to calm down. Instead of yelling about the car, I'd sit back, relax, and say, 'What can I do to help these guys fix this thing? What can I tell them?' Instead of jumping right on the radio, I'd say to myself, 'Let me just ride for a few laps and really figure out what the car is doing.'

"In some races, I did a good job of staying calm, at others, I didn't. At Indianapolis, I just lost my cool. That could have been our race again, but it slipped away and we finished sixth, and I was very frustrated. So I still have my days. But I'm trying."

He measures his increased patience not just by his immediate reactions during bad races, but also by his recovery later on.

"I used to dwell on the bad days, and never get 'em out of my mind, and just be mad at the whole world," Gordon says. "Now it's totally different. By the time I leave the racetrack, I'm usually OK. In fact, I'm the guy who's calming other people down, saying, 'Don't worry about it. We've got next week.'"

The one race in 1995 which took him a long time to get over, he says, was that June event at Pocono, when his restart blunder handed the win to his Hendrick teammate Terry Labonte.

Of all the racers in this early 1990s photo, former Cup champs Bobby Labonte (left) and Jeff Gordon (right) are still full-time. Kenny Wallace (left-middle) and Wally Dallenbach (right of Wallace) now have commentator jobs. *SCR Archives*

"Pocono bothered me because, in this sport, it takes the contribution of a lot of people to make things happen. It takes a team effort. You win together, and you lose together. But in that instance, there was nobody else to blame. It was just . . . *me*. That was a race we should have won, but I messed up."

"Have you missed a shift since that day?"

"No."

He lives, he learns, and he just keeps getting better. There is no telling yet how good he might one day be.

"I'm not saying I'm a smart driver," Gordon says, "but I know I've become smarter. The way I used to drive, the gas pedal was either down, or it was up. I could have just used a switch: on or off. Today, I squeeze into the gas a little easier."

It all comes down to this: "I'm four or five years into stock cars now, and I'm starting to understand what the cars are supposed to feel like, and what the tracks are like, and how they change."

Sounding absolutely serious, the 1995 Winston Cup champion says, "I'm starting to really get comfortable here."

He is talking about racing, but he might just as well be talking about his entire life. Jeff Gordon has never looked more comfortable off the track than he does right now.

"I think there's been a big change in me," he admits.

Although he has six wins at Martinsville, including three straight in 1996–1997, Gordon isn't error-free. He came in too hot and knocked Hut Stricklin off the jack in this stop. *SCR Archives*

It is a confidence thing, and it allowed us to see him in 1995, maybe for the first time, as more than just some fast young kid. As that center-stage spotlight grew brighter, Gordon was willing to let it light up the corners of his personality, and there emerged a picture of a maturing adult. It is, I believe, a confidence born of many things: his newfound status in the sport, his marriage to the former Brooke Sealy, and, perhaps most important to this process, a spiritual awareness which Gordon says "has helped me grow."

He admits that all the religious references that popped up in his victory lane interviews last year were no accident.

"I have always believed in God," he says. "Growing up, I was not at all into any kind of religion, but it was somewhere way, way back there in my mind. What finally brought it out? I don't know. Maybe because of Max Helton and his Motor Racing Outreach services at the track, and listening to other drivers commit their lives to God. I got more and more interested."

A month before his wedding in November of 1994, Gordon decided he wanted to be baptized, something he had missed as a kid. The ceremony was held at the same North Carolina church where his wife had been baptized years earlier, and it was performed by the same minister.

"I never experienced anything like that," he says. "It changes your life. Since that day, I've gotten more and more involved in this thing. It helps me deal with the ups and the downs of racing. It helps me put everything into perspective, and because of that, I can be more focused. And it probably helps me relax."

To listen to him talk is to realize that Jeff Gordon is serious about his faith. And if you have a hard time with that, it's OK. He understands. Gordon says, "I remember when my sister Kim became a born-again Christian. I laughed at her, told her she was crazy. I really thought she was nuts. And now here I am, five or six years later, and I have all of the same strong feelings that she had."

He does not, however, consider himself to be born-again. "I don't put a label on it. My sister lived in California, and I think the born-again thing was a name that people out there hung on it. I'm just a Christian."

Crew chief Ray Evernham's motivational will and message were distilled to the slogan emblazoned on the 1995 Cup champs' chests. *SCR Archives*

MOTOR SPEEDWAY

NAPA 500

Now he shrugs. "I do know this: A lot of my prayers have been answered."

And he takes none of that for granted. Give Gordon this: He is as objective about his life, and about his success, as you would expect any 24-year-old millionaire athlete to be. His life has changed, sure, but his helmet size seems to have remained the same.

He says, "I'll be the first to admit it: I am in a very good situation. There are people out there who say, 'Well, Jeff Gordon's got the best equipment, the best motors, the best crew chief. He *should* be winning.' And my answer is always, 'That's right.' Because I do have the best of everything. I have no trouble admitting that."

On the contrary, he will spend all day singing the praises of those who have helped him reach such dizzying heights.

People like Rick Hendrick: "Rick is not just a great businessman and a great team owner. He's also a great family man and a great all-around guy. He's someone you'd like to pattern your own life after. If it's my choice—and I hope it will be—he's the guy whose car I'd like to drive for the rest of my career."

And crew chief Ray Evernham: "I might not fit in with every crew chief, and probably not every crew chief would fit in with me. But Ray and I, we work very well together. I think I have a pretty good feel for what the car is doing, and I'm able to communicate it

Dale Earnhardt only missed winning his eighth, and third consecutive, Cup title in 1995 to upstart Gordon by 34 points. He gave it a game run: In the final eight races, he had two wins and three seconds, including this win at Atlanta. *SCR Archives*

to Ray, and he can turn that around and give me what I want."

And his two Hendrick Motorsports teammates, Terry Labonte and Ken Schrader: "They've both helped me a lot at different places. Terry is so smooth; you look at the racetracks where he runs good, and they're all tracks where you've got to drive in easy and come out easy. I've gone to him for help, especially at the road courses. And Kenny, gosh, I've been going to him ever since I was in midgets, asking him about different things. When I first started in Winston Cup, Kenny and I would go testing, and I'm sure I was like this nagging little kid in his ear all the time."

He remains sold on Hendrick's "all for one, and one for all" team strategy, despite having to share Evernham's leadership skills with Schrader in 1996. "I've still got him on the weekends," Gordon says.

Besides, he adds, "You know the old saying: you're only as fast as your competition. If our own teammates are some of our best competition, that's going to make our team even better."

Just how much better can his own team can be? "Who knows? Last year at this time, I wouldn't have believed we could make as big a jump as we made in 1995. We're going to strive again to win every race we can, and to win the championship.

"It's going to be tough to repeat. There are going to be more demands on my time than ever before. I know that. And I'm going to deal with it all, one day at a time, the best I can. But what I do on the racetrack is still the most important thing to me."

He gestures around the big shop. "That, and trying to stay within this group of guys. These guys, they are the nucleus of everything that has happened to me."

Gordon talks, in moments like these, like a man aware that success might drag him away from the people and things that mean the most to him. I wonder aloud if he ever worries about losing touch with people, with his family and friends. He answers slowly, drawing out the words: "One thing I've learned is that it's very, very difficult. . . ."

He stops, frowns, and starts again. "I don't know how to put this in a good way, but I'm just going to go ahead and say it anyway because it's the way I feel. It's almost like sometimes, I want to get away from people. You're around people so much, and you're surrounded by racing so much, that sometimes you just want to get away and not be noticed, and not talk about racing, and just enjoy yourself. If you don't get away sometimes, you're gonna go nuts."

He is not so much afraid of losing touch, obviously, as he is resigned to the fact that losing touch is a necessary evil, a price to be paid.

"There are friends, family, people I used to race with, and I think about those people all the time. But as bad as I might want to talk to 'em, just call 'em up, it's something I don't always do. Because, see, the days when I have time to do that are the days when I just want to . . . *get away*."

You know who he sounds like? He sounds like Dale Earnhardt. He could almost be Earnhardt talking about hunting, or Earnhardt talking about cruising the Bahamas aboard his yacht, or Earnhardt talking about kicking back on his ranch, and just . . . *getting away*. Which brings you right back to the notion of this unlikely pair, separated by 20 years and 6 Winston Cup championships, alone together in the glare of stock car racing's center stage.

Gordon tells me about a Sunday in 1994 when he and Earnhardt rode around a track together in a convertible as part of the pre-race introductions: "There were all these boos for him. I kidded him about that, and Dale smiled and said, 'As long as they're making noise, I'm happy.' Now, lately, he's been joking to me that it's a little bit different than it used to be. There's a lot more boos for *me*. Dale says, 'Hey, what's that noise I hear?' "

He has decided, by the way, that Earnhardt is correct: "If we hadn't won any races, if we hadn't been in contention for the championship, they wouldn't have made any noise at all. So the booing, it's all right."

Gordon has learned as Earnhardt had to before him, that once racing builds you up, it tries awfully hard to knock you down. And he can live with that. His words echo. *What's so bad about this?*

Nothing. There is nothing so bad about Jeff Gordon's life, nothing he can't handle.

All summer long, and into the fall of his 1995 championship run, we waited for him to fall apart at center stage, to fold up in the spotlight, to collapse under the weight of, well, Earnhardt. The point chase was on, and Earnhardt was going to out-race him, outsmart him, out-experience him, and then Earnhardt was going to eat him alive. And if all that failed, a nickname—"Wonder Boy," coined, naturally, by Earnhardt—was going to drive Gordon crazy.

Only none of it happened. And so here he is on a rainy Charlotte afternoon, a Winston Cup champion trying to make the best of one more lost day off. He leans into his pinball machine, sends the silver ball off to topple another target, and this, swear to God, is the message which flashes on the Dr. Dude screen: "I am way cool."

And he is. Cool like, you know, Earnhardt. Cool enough for center stage. The hard part, as Dale can tell him, is trying to stay there. Good problem to have, if Jeff Gordon can solve it.

> "If we hadn't won any races, if we hadn't been in contention for the championship, they wouldn't have made any noise at all. So the booing, it's all right."
> —Jeff Gordon

RAY EVERNHAM: CAPTAINING A DYNASTY

BY BOB MYERS
Circle Track, December 1996

Ray Evernham needs no introduction as the crew chief behind defending Winston Cup champion Jeff Gordon and Hendrick Motorsports' remarkable DuPont Chevrolet team. He is a household name in Winston Cup.

Four years ago, few outside of New Jersey had heard of Evernham, including Hendrick Motorsports owner Rick Hendrick. Those who had probably couldn't spell his name. A former modified driver and IROC mechanic from Red Bank, New Jersey, Evernham had little Winston Cup experience, and none in management, when he came to Hendrick in late 1992.

His Winston Cup connection came when he met Andy Petree, a leading crew chief and sometimes driver Phil Barkdoll whose car he prepared for the 1990 Daytona 500. Petree and Barkdoll helped arrange a deal for Evernham to lead a team that would bring Gordon, then at 19 the hottest young driver in the country, to NASCAR and the Busch Grand National Series.

The BGN ride fizzled after two

Crew chief Ray Evernham realized his thwarted driving ambitions by helping mold Gordon's formidable skills to stock cars.
SCR Archives

races, but Evernham was thoroughly convinced that Gordon was for real. Gordon went to Bill Davis' Busch team. Evernham, a chassis specialist, returned to New Jersey, but came back to work for the late Alan Kulwicki in January 1992. Kulwicki and Evernham were constantly at odds, and almost came to blows the day before the Daytona 500.

Evernham quit and was leaving the Daytona Speedway garage when he ran into Preston Miller, Ford Motor Company's Motorsports field manager. Miller asked where he was going. Home, Evernham said. Miller told him that Bill Davis could use him.

By chance, Evernham and Gordon were reunited. The impact was instant: 3 BGN victories, 11 poles that season, and a strong professional and personal bond between driver and crew chief. When Gordon, unprotected by a contract with Ford, signed to drive Rick Hendrick's Winston Cup Chevrolets, he tactfully convinced the owner to hire Evernham.

The Gamble Pays Off

That might well be how Winston Cup's next dynasty was put together. "Rick didn't know Ray," Gordon says, "but was willing to take a chance on a rookie driver and a rookie crew chief. I don't think he is sorry."

Hendrick is, in fact, jubilant. The automobile magnate who owns 75 dealerships says Evernham is a tremendous asset to the organization and that he has been extremely impressed with the systems he has developed, his creativity and multitalents, his ideas toward the future, and his stabilizing effect on Gordon.

Sure, Hendrick Motorsports, something of a slumbering giant at the time, was the largest and richest Winston Cup operation. And Gordon, given the sport's growth since Dale Earnhardt appeared in 1979, was the most ballyhooed yearling in NASCAR annals. Still, what the team—practically all-rookie in 1993—has accomplished under Evernham's leadership is beyond the wildest imagination.

In less than four seasons, the team has reached the highest level, dominated and captivated with the 1995 championship. Hendrick Motorsports, which also fields drivers Terry Labonte and Ken Schrader, has become a triple threat in Winston Cup.

Evernham, 39, says his team, so far, is ahead of schedule. "I didn't expect us to win the championship this soon," he says. "We put a five-year term on that. But the bottom line is we are where we wanted to be. When we started this team, we set out to be to Winston Cup racing what Earnhardt and Childress Racing are. They were the car to beat every race, the best in the business.

"Now, people know that they've got to beat number twenty four too. That's a real satisfying honor because that's the goal we set. Not everyone likes us, but I hope most everyone respects Jeff's and this team's abilities. I'm not saying we are as good as the number three team, but we're coming. What Richard Childress has done through the 1980s and 1990s is a high mark to shoot for."

Sam Sharpe

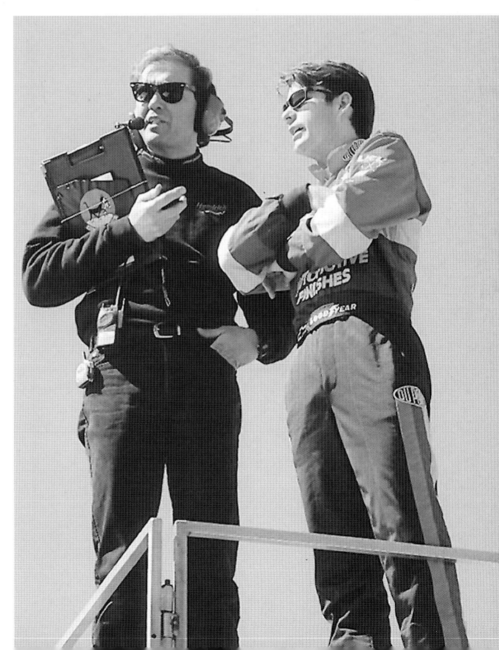

Refuse to Lose

A late-season decline in performance that has characterized the team each season and almost cost it the title in the face of an Earnhardt charge last season won't happen this year, Evernham predicted emphatically at midseason. "We are the best prepared with more cars and engines built than in the team's existence," he says. "We have two more people in the shop and we have a schedule that won't work anybody fourteen weeks in a row.

"We're going to kick rear ends during that last fourteen-race stretch. We may crash and break, but our performance level is not going to slip. That's where our pact, refuse to lose, comes in."

Well, how did his team accomplish so much so quickly and how does he explain the resurgence of Hendrick Motorsports?

Evernham has Hendrick's abundant resources and the phenomenal 25-year-old Gordon, but he firmly believes that attitude defines his team and the resurgence at 120-member Hendrick Motorsports. "I believe that attitude is seventy-five percent of life and it's certainly a big part of this business," Evernham says. "The first twenty cars in the garage have the same stuff. It's how you put it together and use it that makes the difference.

Ed Guzzo's dependable work as chief mechanic has enabled Evernham (shown) to experiment with chassis and aerodynamics, two of his specialties. *Nigel Kinrade*

"We have accomplished, not I. I'm only as good as the people around me, and I'm fortunate from that standpoint. I was at the right place at the right time.

"On the work side, though, it boils down to attitude. Rick Hendrick is a smart man, a visionary, but he can't do everything. In the past, I don't think he has gotten his money's worth. He's always had the resources, but they weren't used properly. It might sound trite, but now he simply has the right people working together, people who believe in the multi-car concept, the open-door policy, the objective, and each other.

"I've always been a competitive person," Evernham continues. "If I can't do my best, I don't want to do it. I want to do this and I want to be the best. I've tried particularly hard to be that. I try to lead by example. If I don't do anything else in life, I hope that some of the example I've set has rubbed off on the people I've had for three or four years."

> *"We're going to kick rear ends during that last 14-race stretch. We may crash and break, but our performance level is not going to slip. That's where our pact, refuse to lose, comes in."*
>
> —Ray Everham

Master of His Domain

Evernham continues to self-improve. He attends motivational and management seminars, reads books by and about successful coaches such as the NBA's Pat Riley and the NFL's late Vince Lombardi, and studies great leaders. One of Evernham's prized possessions is a letter from Riley acknowledging the team's accomplishments. Primary sponsor DuPont sent in a group to study Evernham's teamwork style, for use in its plants.

Signs and placards are displayed on the walls of the team's shops in the Hendrick Motorsports complex near Charlotte Motor Speedway. Some doubt that motivational approach, but they can't argue with the results, Evernham says.

Well-documented publicly over the past three years is a checklist of goals from Riley's book, "The Winner Within: From Upstart to Contender, from Contender to Winner, from Winner to Champion, from Champion to Dynasty." All but the last are checked off. "There's only one team that's checked them all, Earnhardt and Childress Racing," Evernham says. "Give us five more years."

Evernham is tough to work for, but nobody's lashed in stocks. He demands compliance and strives for perfection. His guys come first. He treats them fairly, with dignity and respect, and pays them well. They share a winning percentage of the car and Evernham has gotten them mini-car and T-shirt deals. "Something for being a Rainbow Warrior," he says.

"I used to be the worst manager in the world. I managed too much off my emotions and not enough off my brain. I've learned that you get a lot more out of people if you let them grow. If my people are giving the effort, I'll go to the ends of the world for them."

What did he tell his team after this year's disastrous two-race start? "That we had no control over an accident and engine trouble, that when we finished a race, we'd win. And we did, more than once," Evernham says. "They don't see adversity as such. They simply believe they're going to win, no matter what happens."

Utility Player

Fourteen-hour days at the shop are common for Evernham. His primary responsibility is managing his and Schrader's Budweiser teams. Schrader's outfit, winless since 1991 through the first 22 races this year, was put under the Evernham umbrella this year and restructured—with a broom. Only Schrader and the truck driver remained under the command of crew chief Phil Hammer, promoted from the No. 24 team.

"I'm not hands-on with the number twenty-five team," Evernham says. "Phil runs it. I'm very pleased. Schrader needs to get a whiff of victory again and finish in the top ten in points this year and they'll be all right." The No. 24 team's chief mechanic, Ed Guzzo, has taken a load off Evernham, freeing the crew chief to concentrate on management and organization, and "to fool around" with chassis and aerodynamics.

In fact, Evernham is working on a human resources plan that has nothing to do with cars. "It's inevitable that NASCAR is going to add races," he says. "and I'm trying to figure out how to keep my people motivated and maintain the level of intensity without burning them out when we run thirty-five races a season. Attitude is the key to getting that last check mark—Dynasty—not a slick car body or horsepower. One thing I'm looking at in the next two years is forming a Busch Grand National team, a farm team like in baseball, to do nothing but train people."

Gordon says his crew chief and buddy has made a major impact on his driving and life. "Ray has made me more disciplined, focused, and able to concentrate," Gordon says. "He has calmed me and shown a lot of patience with me. And sometimes I have to calm him down. We believe in each other, trust each other. It's a wonderful relationship.

"If I had my choice, I couldn't see myself driving for another crew chief. And we aren't concerned about that for the near future.

"We could never have accomplished what we have without Ray, and I wouldn't have wanted to try. He means a ton to the team. Hendrick's resources helped start a team of rookies from scratch. But Ray is more than a crew chief. He's a leader, coach, motivator; his dedication and desire rub off on everybody on the team."

Rick Hendrick agrees, "I doubt that the chemistry between Ray and Jeff and their faith in each other could be duplicated. Ray believes that Jeff can do anything once he gets into a race car. We have a similar situation with Terry Labonte and Gary DeHart. I believe our engine program, headed by Randy Dorton, is second to none, and Eddie Dickerson is building some of the best cars I've ever seen. We've put all of that together, and I sure hope the bubble doesn't pop."

"Winning the championship is the best thing that ever happened to Jeff in racing," adds Evernham. "The change is like night and day. He is maturing way faster than anybody ever imagined. He's a seasoned Winston Cup veteran now, and he's acting like it. He's learned what motivates people, knows the importance of his guys. He wants to keep this team together for a long time, and he's doing all the right things to do that."

The Price of Success

Evernham's devotion to racing is taking a toll on his family life, however. His and wife Mary's son, Ray J., 5, has leukemia. Diagnosed on his first birthday, the malady is in remission. "The worst part of this sport is it takes you away from your family," Evernham says. "I've got to figure out a way to resolve that. Maybe they can travel more with me. Everybody in racing pays a price, but I'm at the point I don't want to pay it anymore, so I've got to deal with it.

"Ray J. is doing great. The support the fans have given that little boy, the Leukemia Society, and other charities because of publicity is phenomenal. We've raised a lot of money for the benefit of others and we have other activities planned, especially at the Atlanta race in November."

Evernham might not want always to be a crew chief. He wants to stay with the Hendrick organization a long time, perhaps advancing on the motorsports side of the business, and to be associated with Gordon.

"You've got to give people room to grow," he says. "I've got several people who could fill my shoes." Evernham and Gordon are signed through 2000, as are all of Hendrick's drivers and crew chiefs, including Dorton and Dickerson.

"I've talked with Rick Hendrick about my future and our goals," Evernham says. "Who knows what Rick Hendrick, Jeff Gordon, and Ray Evernham will want to do 10 years from now. Who knows where NASCAR will be?"

"Ray has already moved up as manager of two teams," Hendrick says. "I hope he stays with me as long as I race. In fact, if I can keep all the people I have now, I'd be happy."

Meanwhile, Evernham wants to check off that "Dynasty" notation on the Winston Cup goals list.

Above: Evernham and Gordon share an intensity at the track that is not a put-on. They grew up together at the sport's top level and know the strength of will you need to win. *Sam Sharpe*

Left: Jeff Gordon celebrates his second monumental victory at the Brickyard 400 in August 1998. He was the first to win two there. *SCR Archives*

WHY HENDRICK WINS

**They said a multi-car team would never work.
They didn't understand Rick Hendrick.**

STAFF REPORT
Stock Car Racing, January 1997

Sometimes, the girl nobody paid much attention to in high school shows up at the class reunion looking like a million bucks. It isn't the dress that makes the difference, or the hair, or the shoes because you cannot buy real beauty at the best store in town. The accessories help, but they don't make the package. That took only time. She flits around the room, and all of the guys cannot stop gawking.

If that pretty girl is a race team, she is Hendrick Motorsports. In 1986, when automobile dealer and neophyte car owner Rick Hendrick expanded his modest Winston Cup effort to include a second car—adding Tim Richmond to a team whose only previous driver had been Geoff Bodine—few in the NASCAR fraternity gave him a shot at success. Multi-car teams, generally speaking, had not worked in stock car racing, and Hendrick's outfit hardly seemed likely to reverse that trend. While there were the bright spots—Bodine's victory in the 1986 Daytona 500, Richmond's six-win season that same year—there certainly wasn't the kind of overwhelming success that sent opposing owners scrambling to build larger teams.

But just look at Hendrick Motorsports today. Two of its drivers, Jeff Gordon and Terry Labonte, fought down to the wire for the 1996 Winston Cup championship, which was decided at Atlanta. In the last two seasons, Rick Hendrick has dominated big-league NASCAR racing like no other owner in recent memory. His three-car team—the Kellogg's 5 of Labonte, the DuPont 24 of Gordon, and the Budweiser 25 driven in 1996 by Ken Schrader and to be driven in 1997 by Ricky Craven—is the envy of the sport. It took only time.

"This is not something that happened overnight," says Gary DeHart, Labonte's crew chief.

And it is not something that was built with welders, wrenches, or milling machines. Those who see the Hendrick edge as purely mechanical—owing to superior engines, bodies, and/or chassis designs—are clearly missing the mark. The accessories help, but they don't make the package. The success of Hendrick Motorsports is rooted in flesh and bone and brains.

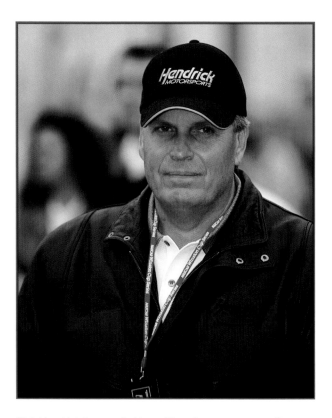

Rick Hendrick has made his multi-car team a success. Some think the key is simply the sheer numbers of the multi-car concept. But not everyone who has tried running several teams has had much success at it. *SCR Archives*

Hendrick Motorsports standardized production processes at its mammoth complex. The individual teams adapt the basic hardware to their driver's style. *SCR Archives*

Listen to Gordon's crew chief, Ray Evernham, who since joining the Hendrick fold to assemble Gordon's team has become a garage area superstar: "Rick always had good equipment. It's just that now, he's got the right combination of people."

And DeHart: "The people are what make the difference."

And Labonte: "Rick Hendrick went out and got good people, the right people, and he's kept them."

And Darrell Waltrip, a former Hendrick Motorsports driver: "Rick Hendrick is a people person."

Are you starting to notice a theme here?

Right from the start, Hendrick knew people better than he knew racing. Oh, his father, affectionately called Papa Joe, had owned modified coupes years ago, and the younger Hendrick was a lifelong stock car enthusiast. But what he knew best was people; specifically, how to sell them cars. It had made him a rich man, and he ventured into NASCAR in 1984 with a rich man's zeal.

Labonte, who watched all this from a distance while winning the 1984 Winston Cup title with another team, says, "Rick obviously had a pretty good idea of what he wanted to do."

Pretty good, indeed. "I related racing to the automobile business," Hendrick says. In his nationwide string of nearly 90 dealerships, he had learned that by "being able to share information, we were more successful." He could think of no real reason why the same theory wouldn't work in NASCAR, where his lone team had been a winner early on with Bodine. Hendrick recalls that when he was approached with a sponsorship package for 1986 based on a second team, his reaction was, "This makes sense. We need to do this."

Today, people up and down pit road cite all kinds of reasons why multi-car teams are the coming rage in Winston Cup racing, and maybe in the Busch Series too. One is NASCAR's rule limiting the number of private test sessions per car; Hendrick's three-car squad can go testing three times as often, and bring home three times the data, as, say, Rusty Wallace's single-car team. But when Hendrick hired Richmond in 1986, testing was the furthest thing from his mind. What sparked his entrepreneurial imagination were the possibilities for pooling resources and manpower.

The thinking is not complicated: Two teams, properly financed, bring in twice the sponsorship dollars, but do not automatically require twice the infrastructure. In other words, you don't necessarily need twice as many engine builders, or twice as many chassis jigs, or twice as many men shaping fenders, or even twice as many secretaries answering the phones.

Waltrip simplifies all this by declaring, "It takes the same level of organization to run three teams as it does to run one team, but with three teams you can triple your resources. Rick saw the value in that way back when."

The math applies to human, as well as financial, resources. DeHart says, "The more people you've got sharing notes and knowledge, the better off you are. You might end up with the same information a smaller team ends up with, but you'll get it quicker."

Hendrick's brightest move may have been the creation of shared fabrication and engine shops. In the cases of certain other

The road to multi-car success wasn't easy or paved with trophies. Although Darrell Waltrip won the Daytona 500 and several other races with Waddell Wilson as his crew chief and Rick Hendrick the car owner, Hendrick admits that what was termed the "Dream Team" didn't achieve as much as its members had hoped for. *SCR Archives*

multi-car failures, car owners simply created two complete teams which operated independently; in effect, the overall team doubled in size, but not in efficiency.

"The multi-car [sponsorship] numbers gave us an opportunity to have specialists," Hendrick says. "I look at it like, if you have a problem with your foot, you don't go to a neurosurgeon, you go to a specialist. We developed [specialists] in the body department, the chassis department, and the motor department."

And little by little, even as Hendrick Motorsports struggled, there began to emerge this notion of unity. Gordon says, "Rick was able to show every single person on his teams that working together could pay off. They saw, 'Hey, we can benefit from the resources that are here.' And because of that, they don't mind working together."

The inability to work together had been the Achilles heel of most of the mega-teams that had preceded Hendrick's. In the 1960s, when Detroit's automobile manufacturers spent gobs of money loading their rosters with name drivers, the one thing they could not buy was team spirit. Two decades later, in 1985, Bobby Allison was so angered when his DiGard Racing owners began fielding a second car that

he left the team with which he had won the Winston Cup championship just two seasons earlier.

And even as Rick Hendrick began his two-car experiment, he only had to look across the garage area to see the kind of trouble he had let himself in for. The legendary Junior Johnson, thought by many to have a personality strong enough to make a two-car team work through

This is exactly the idea, Hendrick cars running at the top. The premise is to get the right people together and then supply them with top equipment. The results are undeniable. *SCR Archives*

sheer will, instead was watching one of his drivers (Waltrip) blow off the other (Neil Bonnett) on a near-weekly basis.

Waltrip says, "Remember, there weren't the parts available that you have now. For example, it's hard, even today, to build two exactly equal engines; it's hard to build two equal anything. But when I was with Junior, it was impossible. Today, with computerized machinery [producing matched components], everyone can have equipment that's pretty close. Back then, you always had one engine that was better than the rest. One week you might get it, and the next week your teammate might get it. So what happened was, you'd end up with one good car and one mediocre car."

Hendrick's contention was that a multi-car team that truly functioned as a team, sharing technology and the aforementioned specialists, would eventually succeed where others had failed.

"I took an awful lot of heat back in the late 1980s and early 1990s," he recalls. "So many times in the garage area, I would be told, 'You'll never win a championship with a multi-car team. You can't do it.' But we just continued on with our plan."

And Hendrick was as patient as he was persistent. DeHart says, "In my opinion, most people who tried multi-car teams didn't try 'em long enough. It took Rick years and years of moving people around to see how they would work together."

Hendrick says, "From the very beginning, I was committed—we were committed, as an organization—to make it work."

He thinks he came close to having "the right chemistry" a few times: first with Bodine and Richmond, and then with two different three-car teams: Bodine, Waltrip, and Schrader, and then Gordon, Schrader, and Ricky Rudd. "But every time I got the chemistry about where it needed to be, something happened," Hendrick says. First Richmond fell sick with AIDS, from which he later died; then Waltrip and Rudd left to form their own teams. But while all of these changes were clearly setbacks, they did help clear the way for the trio—Schrader (who arrived in 1988), Gordon (1993), and Labonte (1994)—which has carried Hendrick Motorsports to its greatest heights.

"A lot of things have changed since I was there," Geoff Bodine (right) says of Rick Hendrick's operation. "When it became a multi-car team, it hadn't matured enough." *SCR Archives*

There was considerable opportunity for Rick Hendrick to visit victory lane in 1997: 10 times. He also got to sit at the head table at the awards banquet for the second time with Gordon as his driver. *SCR Archives*

"Some of the guys who were with Rick earlier—and I won't call anyone names—were just a little bit bullheaded," DeHart says.

And some of them simply had the bad timing to come along before Hendrick's grand scheme could be realized. Bodine, for one, knows he showed up too early. "A lot of things have changed since I was there. When it became a multi-car team, it hadn't matured enough; we didn't have the resources to support a team that big. The engine program wasn't solid, the chassis program was hit-or-miss. I left just when they were starting to get things together."

Gordon's timing, on the other hand, was perfect, and he knows it. "I benefited from all the years that other people put in to make this team what it is. Not many rookies come into Winston Cup with the engine program, the chassis program, the resources that I had."

By 1993, when Gordon arrived, there was no denying that the multi-car concept was on the verge of arriving. And ever since, those team owners with less foresight and less guts than Rick Hendrick showed back in 1986 have spent an awful lot of Sundays watching his cars run circles around theirs.

Evernham says, "All those people who said multi-car teams couldn't work, they're just like the people who said running a rear sway bar couldn't work until we showed them it could. Multi-car teams can work; they've worked in Formula One and in Indy cars for years. There was no reason why they couldn't work here too. Rick knew that, and he stuck to his guns. That's the biggest reason this whole thing turned around: He was willing to see his vision through."

Hendrick, who would never pay himself that kind of compliment, does allow himself a small boast when he sees the copycat effect his success has wrought. Jack Roush added a third team in 1996; Richard Childress will run two cars next season; Felix Sabates seems set to operate three teams; and there is talk that down the road, Kranefuss-Haas and Penske South might field second cars.

"All of a sudden," Hendrick grins, "multi-car teams are the way to go."

His grin, mind you, is not mere self-congratulation. Hendrick seems amused by the thought that some of his fellow car owners are about to walk a mile in his shoes. The fit, he says, might not be comfortable. "If [those teams] don't have the right chemistry, it won't work."

Evernham agrees: "If you don't get the right people, it would hurt you rather than help you. People see that you can do a second team cheaper because of resources and things like that, but if you don't have people who will work together, it'll cost you more money because you won't succeed."

DeHart says that any car owner trying to emulate Hendrick Motorsports will need "cooperation from everybody involved on both teams, or all three teams, or however many they have."

And as all of this unfolds, the two happiest guys in the garage area might be Labonte and Gordon. Each is coming off a spectacular 1996 and enters the coming season with an unchanged team, while much of the opposition goes through growing pains.

"I don't think going to multi-car teams will be as easy as people think," Labonte says. "I think it's going to be a setback for some of them. Because, I'll tell you, if you don't have people with the right attitude about being on a multi-car team, it's just not going to work.

"I've heard comments made by drivers who don't like the thought of being on a multi-car team, but I came here with the attitude that 'I am going to make this work to my advantage.' If you go in there unhappy, things probably aren't going to go too good."

Gordon says, "If other teams try this and they don't work together, I guarantee you they'll fail. If they start worrying just about beating their teammates, that's only going to cause confusion and chaos and tear down their teams instead of building them up."

One of the credos Hendrick lives by is, "All good businesses are torn down from the inside." He says, "I believe that more in racing than in any other business I've ever been associated with."

With that in mind, he is vigilant about keeping Hendrick Motorsports bonded from the inside out. He demands that all of his teams get equal treatment from the engine and fabrication shops. He brings his crew chiefs together regularly—"We meet every Tuesday"—to discuss the race just completed and the race to come. He has devised a season-end bonus program through which "everybody in our organization is compensated [according to] the overall efforts of all our teams." The program, Hendrick says, ensures that "two hundred people are motivated to see those cars do well." All of this is designed to avoid the petty jealousies that threaten any multi-car team.

That's not to say that everything is always sugar and spice at Hendrick Motorsports. DeHart says, "I'm not going to sit here and say that some of our team members and drivers over the years haven't been jealous about certain things."

"That sort of thing goes on a little bit," Evernham admits. "But you've got to get over it. It's not like one guy's got new cars and new engines, and the other guy doesn't."

Gordon says, "I'm sure that what's kept some guys out of Rick's cars is that they think the other guy is going to get the best stuff. But there really is no best stuff."

His teammate and 1996 championship rival concurs. "When I took this ride," Labonte says, "people told me, 'You're making a mistake. Jeff's there, and Kenny's been there for a long time. You're going to get all the leftovers.' Well, that's been so far from the truth. Everything at Hendrick is first-class. We all have good cars, good engines, and good people. The stuff is just so close."

But it wasn't always this way. To hear Geoff Bodine tell it, the early days of the Hendrick expansion weren't a whole lot different than, say, Waltrip's two-car experience with Junior Johnson.

"People were getting mad at each other, jealous of each other," Bodine says. "We knew there wasn't enough good stuff to go around, and everyone wanted the good stuff for themselves. And when my engine parts ended up on somebody else's car and they ran fast while my engine broke, I really got a bad taste for multi-car teams."

Top: Says Ray Evernham, "All those people who said multi-car teams couldn't work, they're just like the people who said running a rear sway bar couldn't work until we showed them it could." *SCR Archives*

Above: Hendrick has research and construction resources second to none, but its "soul" originates from people like "Papa Joe" Hendrick (Rick's father), sharing victory with Gordon and crew at Martinsville in 1997. *SCR Archives*

Right: Gordon and Hendrick share some male bonding time while wife Brooke looks on. *SCR Archives*

But it was a period Rick Hendrick learned from. And the lesson was this: "You have to have an open relationship."

Hendrick says, "The way we've got it designed, there's no way you could favor one guy with an engine. The same area does the machine work [for all three teams]. They'll do 20 sets of pistons at one time, 10 sets of rods at one time. The cams are ground at the same time. Our cylinder heads are done on a CNC machine, so they're identical. The parts then go to an assembler, and each team does have its own assembler. And when [the engines] get to the dyno and they run, there might be a three to five horsepower difference, but that's it. The motors are that close."

If anyone has doubts, from driver to crew chief, Hendrick has a simple solution: "Show 'em the dyno sheets."

Occasionally, Hendrick admits, one car might have a bigger edge in power "for maybe one race." This occurs, he says, when that team's engine builder has an idea, does the required testing, and decides to risk trying it in a race. But he insists, as soon as there are enough such pieces to go around, "we're going to share it."

As for the cars run by the individual teams, Hendrick allows that small things—he uses steering boxes as an example—often differ because "each driver wants a little different feel." But the basic frames and the way they are built, he says, "are identical." He points out that sometimes a car originally built for Team A will go instead to Team B if a crash has left Team B's driver short on the proper equipment. "We'll give his team that car," Hendrick says.

Labonte, a man not given to overstatement, says, "Our engines are so close, you wouldn't believe it. I could walk over right now and get a spare engine from the 24 truck or the 25 truck, put it in my car, and not be able to tell the difference from whatever engine is in there now. It's the same with the cars; my guys could switch to the backup car at night, and if they didn't tell me, I would not know it."

"Rick does it the way McDonald's does," Waltrip says. "If you eat a quarter-pounder with cheese in Charlotte, it'll be the same as a quarter-pounder with cheese you eat in Nashville. His cars are the same, and his engines are the same."

And they have been refined to the point where they often look like the best cars and engines in the sport, thanks to an information-sharing system unparalleled in NASCAR history. Even Hendrick is impressed by the lengths to which his team has taken his all-for-one marching orders. He speaks proudly of weekends when "at eleven o'clock at night, Gary DeHart and Ray Evernham are in the same [motel] room sharing notes because one of their cars is struggling."

DeHart says, "We've learned things at different tracks from the twenty-four car and the twenty-five car, and sometimes they've learned from us. We'll help each other all we can."

Does that help have its limits? Naturally. "We don't share everything," Evernham says with a smile. "It's kind of like if you're bowling or golfing with your kid brother. You'll help him beat everybody else, but you really don't want him to beat you.

"We'll help each other, but we're not going to give our top-secret stuff to, say, the five car, and they're not going to give us theirs. And nobody expects that because neither one of us has really been struggling. But lately, we've both been helping the twenty-five car because they have been struggling."

Ah, the paradox of "the 25 car." On one hand, Schrader's long winless streak—dating back to 1991—served to point out that Hendrick Motorsports is not infallible. On the other hand, the slump ironically underscored the team's togetherness. Think about it: This is a three-car team in which two run up front regularly and one does not. The same situation could have torn apart a less-cohesive unit. Yet even when Schrader left Hendrick Motorsports at season's end and Ricky Craven took his place, the transition was smooth and without controversy.

"Rick Hendrick and I have a good relationship," Schrader said in announcing his decision to leave. "I've been with him nine years, and that's a long time in this business."

NASCAR'S LEADING MAN

Racing's Got a Tiger of Its Own

BY BOB MYERS
Circle Track, September 1997

Like Tiger Woods, Jeff Gordon came into his sport challenging and beating the old guard almost from the start. *SCR Archives*

On that memorable day in April 1997 when Tiger Woods romped through the Masters, changing the history of professional golf, the thought occurred to me of the striking similarities between golfing's rookie phenom and NASCAR Winston Cup driving sensation, Jeff Gordon.

At 21, Woods, an African- and Asian-American, is stirring up professional golf as perhaps no other at a time when the sport is truly in need of a superstar and his glitter. Woods won five of his first 16 PGA tournaments and exceeded $2 million in earnings, playing to record crowds and television audiences, creating "Tiger-mania" and a media blitz. Some predict Woods to become bigger than Michael Jordan, whom he refers to as "big brother." Companies such as Nike, Titlelist, and American Express, whose sponsorships total $86 million, believe he will transcend the sport and become known beyond the realm of golf worldwide.

Gordon, who turns 26 in August and has had a four-year headstart, has done activities in NASCAR and Winston Cup comparable to what Woods is doing for golf. His impact, however, hasn't been as great as Woods'. Winston Cup still glowed in the brilliance of Dale Earnhardt and had more major stars than golf when Gordon cracked the big league at 21 in 1993. Racing was robust and healthy when Gordon arrived, so it's difficult to assess how much he has helped boost the ever-increasing attendance and television ratings and helped grow the sport over five years.

To be sure, nobody has accomplished as much as quickly and at such a young age as Gordon has in Winston Cup. He already has one championship, a runner-up, 23 victories, and more than $11 million in earnings, as of this writing. Like it or not, driving for Hendrick Motorsports, he has set the standard and carries the torch. Coming in as the next Earnhardt, he has far-exceeded his billing and most people's imaginations. Predictably and perceptibly, he has gotten better. Including his winless rookie year, Gordon won 17 percent of his first 134 starts, but a whopping 27.4 percent with a total of 17 victories in 1995 and 1996. Winning 5 of the first 11 this year, he's been on a pace to exceed last year's 10 victories (and win the Winston Million-dollar bonus if he wins the Southern 500 at Darlington on August 31).

No Color Barrier

Knowing Gordon up close, and Woods from a distance—based upon what's been seen, heard, and read—there appear to be similarities other than both possessing gifted talent. They're both good-looking, personable, charming, and articulate. They have a lot of humility, a redeeming quality in their respective positions. Though mature beyond their years, they both possess a youthful innocence—such that unless you're a competitor whose just gotten his butt beat or are a fan of a rival, you want to hug them. They project the image—genuine, I believe—that makes those who want a piece of them drool. And you wouldn't believe how many there are in that number.

Truly, Woods and Gordon are the faces of the future in their sports, and shame on us if it matters that Woods' face is black. If that dark chapter in golf's history (when blacks were excluded from the PGA and, until 1990, denied membership in most country clubs) hadn't ended thanks to such pioneers as Charlie Sifford and Lee Elder and to Woods, it has now.

Elder was quoted in an article in Fortune after the Masters, "after this, no one will turn their head when they see a black man walk to a tee." The potential for Woods and Gordon to impact the competitive and business sides of their sports as role models, and to inspire those of all walks and colors—especially youngsters—to play golf and race is mind-boggling. And Gordon is just entering what's considered a racer's prime as other big names slip into the twilight.

There are almost no blacks in NASCAR Winston Cup racing—including drivers, car owners, or crewmen—and, with few exceptions, the sport has been all-white. Hence, there are few blacks among the record crowds attending races. The late Wendall Scott, who raced in the early 1960s and early 1970s, could have been a pioneer for his race if he had had the means. In 1978, Humpy Wheeler, president of Charlotte Motor Speedway, invited Willy T. Ribbs, a promising young open-wheel driver

> *It appears that Gordon and Woods came out of nowhere and became overnight sensations. Truth is, they've "done their things" since childhood. Perhaps the most striking similarity is the time invested in them by their parents, who gave them attention, guidance, and direction, and seem to have done everything right.*

"Surround yourself with good people." The 1990 crew: *(from left)* Charlie Waters, Marty Sweeting, Gordon, Andy Graves (future crew chief and team manager in Cup), and Bickford. *SCR Archives*

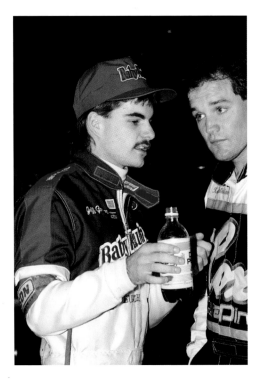

to race in the 600; but it didn't happen. A flap developed over a deal for a car, and Ribbs got arrested for driving the wrong way on a one-way street in downtown Charlotte. Ribbs came back a second time, joining a team, DiGard Racing, that had deteriorated so badly it wasn't competitive. "Willy T. had a lot of potential," says Wheeler, "and I think if he had started in 1978 and stuck with it, he would have made it and maybe attracted other minorities."

Why are there no black drivers in NASCAR'S big league? Only a small percentage of Americans of any color can afford to get into racing or even the opportunity. "Right now I don't see a Tiger Woods on the horizon," adds Wheeler, "although he might still be in a high chair or running a short track in California. We could handle it because things in our sport have changed significantly in the past 10 to 15 years and it could happen."

Indeed it could. In May, former NBA great Julius "Dr. J." Erving and NFL star Joe Washington, both black, announced that they will organize a Winston Cup team to debut in 1998. Washington Erving Motorsports will be the first minority-owned and operated team in NASCAR since Scott retired in 1975.

Child Prodigy

Gordon didn't spring into Cup victory circles without plenty of wheel time in open wheel cars. Kenny Wallace gets some tips here. SCR Archives

It appears that Gordon and Woods came out of nowhere and became overnight sensations. Truth is, they've "done their things" since childhood. Perhaps the most striking similarity is the time invested in them by their parents, who gave them attention, guidance, and direction, and seem to have done everything right. Oh, Woods' African-American father, Earl, and his Asian mother, Kultida, did make a miscue of sorts from the onset when they named their son Eldrick. But Earl, a former Green Beret and an avid golfer at the time, quickly recouped, choosing the sobriquet "Tiger" (after a buddy in the Vietnam War).

John Bickford, Gordon's stepfather, and his mother Carol did not script the child to be a race car driver, as perhaps did Earl Woods when he put a golf club in his toddler's hands. "Everybody wants to believe that," Bickford says. "I'd love to say that and have everybody's dreams come true like a fairy tale, but it's not the story." Though they had little money and often worked two jobs, the Bickfords, who lived in Vallejo, California, managed to give their son the opportunity to race at an early age and saw that he was good at it. They built him equipment better than most, and he raced some more—and he was exceptional. At some point he had to get a job, so he chose to work at what he did best.

When Gordon was four years old, he joined the kids on the block racing bicycles; but he was so tiny, a mere 30 pounds, that his parents feared injury. Bickford bought a couple of old quarter midget cars out of a barn and rebuilt them. "Jeff went crazy when he saw the cars and promptly jumped into one," recalls Bickford.

Bickford got permission to carve-out a small track at the county fairgrounds—part dirt, part asphalt, and part weeds. Gordon, then five, spun out practically every lap for three hours before he got the hang of it. He has been on competitive wheels ever since. The youngster turned literally thousands of laps in that field of dreams, burning up motor after motor for Bickford to rebuild, before his first organized race at a dirt track in Sacramento. Bickford realized a second childhood through his stepson.

"The difference between race drivers is laps and the ability to control emotions," Bickford says. "A lap at age five is the same quality as a lap at twenty-nine. I'll argue that to my death. I'm not too sure you can't teach a kid at five how to do things better than at twenty-nine. There are no distractions, your total

concentration is on racing, or whatever you're doing. Jeff had superb hand-eye coordination, learned rapidly, and developed a rhythm. We worked on all of that."

The foundation of Gordon's career was laid over eight years in quarter midgets, and everything else has been a building block leading to the top. He ran hundreds of races, twice practically every weekend in a stretch of four years. While he developed and honed his skills, he learned discipline, patience and, most of all, how to be professional. Critics charged that the Bickfords were abusing the kid. When he went to the larger, more powerful sprint cars at 13, people laughed at him because he was so little and an owner wouldn't sell Bickford a car. "My parents pushed me to be the best I could be," Gordon says, "but they never forced me to do anything. I loved racing." The Bickfords didn't yell at or spank their kids. "When Jeff did something wrong, I'd tell him I was disappointed in him, that he was a lot smarter than that and then I'd walk away," Bickford adds. "That would just kill him. He'd say, 'Why don't you yell at me, why don't you hit me, why don't you do something?' I'd say only stupid people do that and that I was intelligent, he was intelligent, and that I wasn't going to treat him otherwise. . . . I didn't lecture to him. I'd paint him a mental picture and let him make decisions. I'd listen to what he said, although at seven, he said little. He was so shy he wouldn't kiss the trophy girl. I think Jeff's whole life has been about trying to be professional in everything he does."

But there were a few rules in the formative years. From the onset, Gordon wore a racing uniform and had his name on his helmet and jacket. "Perception is important," Bickford says. "If you look, act, walk, and quack like a duck, you'll be perceived as a duck." One time when Gordon forgot his helmet and his parents wouldn't allow him to borrow one. Bickford drove nearly three hours to retrieve it while an embarrassed Gordon answered questions as to why he couldn't practice. He never forgot his helmet again.

Gordon's car control was immediately immaculate in Cup, but his crew was also raised the bar with their consistent jaw-dropping, and seconds-dropping, stops. *Nigel Kinrade*

Jeff Gordon's victories helped propel NASCAR's media coverage to a new nationwide level in the 1990s. *SCR Archives*

NASCAR had a media story goldmine that played across the country: Your skilled but underdog young brother against wily veterans and their experience. What wasn't to like? *SCR Archives*

Gordon had a hot temper. "He'd get mad at competitors and make them crash without an obvious clue he'd done anything," Bickford says. "When he came off the track mad, I'd grab him, ask him calmly to put his helmet and gloves in his car and go out of public view to a shed or building and kick and scream and cry to regain his composure, come back to his car, and conduct himself in a professional manner."

When Gordon was six, Bickford put in a no-contact rule. If he made contact that was his fault with another car and won the race, he had to give the trophy and apologize to the competitor he bumped—without crying. "It only took about three trophies, and Jeff learned how to pass cleanly and to screw up his competitors so badly without contact that they didn't know what was happening," Bickford says.

Intimidation, Resentment, Jealousy

A 21-year-old phenom, black or white, who captivates a sport as Woods is doing, and as Gordon has done, fosters intimidation, resentment, and jealousy among the establishment. While it's largely unexpressed at the highest levels, the racially insensitive "fried chicken and collard greens" remark made by veteran pro Fuzzy Zoeller after Woods had won the Masters is an example. The remark was more likely a slam on Woods' feat and how good he is rather than intended as a racial "slur," but it irked the youngster, was out of bounds, and an unlikely joke.

Woods and Gordon have been through that before. They've paid their dues. Woods was not allowed to play on some courses, was chased off others, and says he has received hate mail. Gordon was kicked out of some races or banned from certain classes because he was too good, though the excuses were that he was too experienced, too little, or too aggressive. Usually the youngest and smallest guy in the fastest car, he's stepped on egos and toes for years.

He has learned to handle resentment with humility, expressing awe at his accomplishments and praising the competition he drubs. "I haven't personally seen the jealousy and resentment in Winston Cup," Gordon says, "but I know it's there, and I expected it to be." Fans boo Gordon because he has beaten their favorite—especially Earnhardt—so often, but he says Earnhardt told him not to worry so long as fans react in some manner. "If a minority star emerged in NASCAR," says Wheeler, "he'd have to decide what was intimidation and what was prejudice. If he couldn't understand the difference, then he'd need to go elsewhere because anytime anybody comes into Winston Cup, I don't care who they are or where they're from, and tries to break into what I call 'the club,' there's going to be intimidation." Woods is determining the difference now; Gordon already knows.

Gordon "elbows up" at treacherous Springfield in 1990. After racing open wheel cars with 600 horsepower, what could be intimidating about a stock car?
SCR Archives

Woods says a loss of privacy is his biggest hangup, that he wants to be a normal 21-year-old and have fun playing golf. "I can relate to Tiger," Gordon says, "and all that he is going through. There are some days I'd really like to be an average guy who can go places and not have anybody know me or stare at me, although that's not a particular bother. But it's definitely a major adjustment. I'd like to meet and play golf with Tiger." That will happen and, as you might surmise, Gordon is an excellent golfer for the time he invests in the sport.

No one knows better than John and Carol Bickford the high price of fame. Though they reside only a few miles away, they rarely see their son. "The thing that disappoints me most is not being able to participate anymore," says John Bickford, 50, "and that professional racing takes so much time. Jeff was raised in an environment of helping others and it's hard for him to say no. He does a lot of things he doesn't have to do because that's his nature. He wants to take NASCAR to the highest level."

Carol Bickford says the ride would have been worth it, though, no matter what her son did, whether or not he was famous. She says that parents have an obligation and responsibility to give their children guidance and direction, lest they search and wander aimlessly.

"I owe my whole career to John and my mom," Gordon says. We're not familiar with the methods and tactics Earl Woods used to shape his son's career, or how tough he was on him as a child, but we suspect that Tiger would say the same if that touching, tearful embrace of his father after the Masters was any indication.

"I wouldn't be a race car driver if not for John; and Mom made a lot of sacrifices too," Gordon adds. "My parents were my role models and they set a lot of examples. They opened my eyes to a lot of things, but racing always kept my attention."

And now, as he rewrites the record books, and fans and drivers talk about him incessantly (good and bad), Jeff Gordon certainly has captured the full attention of the racing world.

Gordon's early winning performances at Daytona in the qualifiers were the first indications that the kid was "for real" in Cup circles. *SCR Archives*

THE CHAMPION FANS BOO

STAFF REPORT
Stock Car Racing, March 1998

Jeff Gordon seems to have it all. He's young (26 years old), enormously successful (two Winston Cup championships and 29 Winston Cup race wins in the past four years enough?), married to a drop-dead beautiful woman, and he's drop-dead handsome himself. His annual income is measured in millions.

Last year, Gordon won 10 races—more than anyone else—plus the Winston and the Busch Clash. He also won Winston's million-dollar bonus at Darlington.

He didn't do it alone. Gordon is powered by the enormous resources of Hendrick Motorsports, which provide him with fast engines and cars that handle. Race after race, nobody performs at a consistently high level more than the Rainbow Warriors, his pit crew. His crew chief, Ray Evernham, is considered by many the best in today's Winston Cup. Funding behind the operation appears unlimited.

The guy's even lucky. Gordon's performance last year was highlighted by some spectacular good fortune, which started at the Daytona 500. Remember when his tire went down and Gordon nearly lost a lap? Perhaps it was bad luck to have suffered the tire failure, but it was surely good luck that he got a caution just in time to stay on the lead lap. He went on to win the race. Then there was the Southern 500 when he bounced off the wall, but still won the race. He also bounced off the wall early in the second Rockingham race, and he finished fourth there. The jack dropped prematurely at the Coke 600 at Charlotte, damaging his left front fender, but Gordon soldiered on to win the rain-shortened event. Gordon squeaked through in the final race of the year, despite driving a poorly handling backup car. He just managed to nail down enough points to win the championship over hard chargers Dale Jarrett and Mark Martin, who finished second and third in not only the points but also the race.

After finishing second to teammate Terry Labonte in 1996 by just 37 points (even though he had 10 wins!), Gordon regained the crown in 1997. *SCR Archives*

"I mean, like The Winston Million was really cool, but the third Southern 500 in a row was just as cool." *SCR Archives*

"It would mean a lot to win Sears Point." *SCR Archives*

Gordon didn't get any free passes on track, though. *SCR Archives*

If there is a reason for Gordon's success, it is quite simply that everything works together.

Yet this is an imperfect world. In most sports, fans cheer the winners; but in racing they boo the biggest winner of the past three years. At every race, the introduction of Jeff Gordon produces an unpleasant grandstand refrain as fans loudly express their displeasure. Malicious stories have been hatched and circulated by the kind of people who love to hate a winner.

It cannot be easy to stand before nearly 200,000 people and hear as many boos as Gordon does. It cannot be easy to hear the vicious stories.

Even the upside of success can be trying. In contrast to those who boo or delight in fileting a legend, thousands of cheering fans want Jeff Gordon's autograph and want to have their picture taken with him. Corporations seek his endorsement. Entrepreneurs and thugs alike fancy him as their business partner. It cannot be easy to have the constant pressure of so many people tugging on his arm looking for his time and attention. There is no relief because Gordon's face and success are so well known everywhere.

As the 1997 season wound down, Gordon sat in his race car transporter for an extended one-on-one interview with *Stock Car Racing* magazine editor Dick Berggren. Some of his comments surprised even us.

Youth is a wonderful thing, but not many young people stand atop their profession. What is it like to be 26 and in this situation?

I don't even think about age anymore. Winning races and being competitive—just being at this level in the sport is exciting. I guess because I've always raced against older guys and I've always been the young guy, I stopped thinking about that. I always thought about getting the experience. Now when I sit back and think about it, I know I've got quite a bit of experience at a young age. But I am getting old—especially hanging around with Ray Evernham.

> *"I feel so comfortable
> behind the wheel of the race car.
> That is the one thing that I do in life
> that I feel like I do well."*
>
> —Jeff Gordon

When you look at some of the older guys, like Darrell Waltrip and Dale Earnhardt, some of the drivers in their 40s and beyond, do you ever imagine what it would be like for you to be in your 40s and still racing big-league stock cars?

I really admire those guys because they can go out and still be competitive. I know the wear and tear my body goes through in a 500- or 600-mile race. Sometimes I get out of the car and I'm just whipped. I think, "Man, how do Earnhardt, Marcis, and Darrell do that?" You've got to admire them. I would love to be able to be as competitive as they are at that age. That's what is going to keep me racing at that age, being competitive. I can't see myself riding around just because I can make the races.

There's got to be a point when I move on. I feel like life begins around 40. Racing has been everything to me, but I think and wonder what I'm going to do when I'm not driving a race car or what would I do if I couldn't drive a race car. I've started experiencing the business life, and what happens in licensing and investments and that stuff. I can't wait for the day when I have time to go into an office, my office, and actually sit down and work behind a desk. I mean, I don't want to do that every day of the week, but I think that would be kind of cool.

You've won so many races. Is it still a thrill to drive into victory lane or is it just another race, just another time to swap hats and answer questions?

Oh, no, that is the big thrill for me, to drive into victory lane. Some races do mean more than others, like Daytona, The Brickyard. Everything brings on a different meaning as you go on. I mean, like The Winston Million was really cool, but the third Southern 500 in a row was just as cool.

Winning the Coca Cola 600 [last] year because I changed to Pepsi was big. I mean, that was a big deal because I made a move. I committed myself to a company in return to have them commit themselves to me. To go out there and have a year like we've had and to do that meant a lot to me because I [had] said to Pepsi, "This is why I told you back in January or February that we needed to be together." It meant a lot to me to win at Watkins Glen, a road course, and it would mean a lot to win at Sears Point. The California race: I had a lot of friends and family out there because I'm from California. I wanted to win that race. I mean, I want to win every race, but there are some that mean more than others, for silly reasons sometimes and sometimes for meaningful reasons. Not just money reasons.

You've got so many things that you can do in your present situation. What gives you the greatest pleasure?

I enjoy being Jeff Gordon and the life I lead. There's the career-and-racing side of my life, and then there's a family-and-friends, away-from-the-racetrack life. When you talk about racing and my career, then of course just being able to get out there and drive that race car and to be able to show myself some days that I can do some pretty amazing things behind the wheel of the race car. I feel so comfortable behind the wheel of the race car. That is the one thing that I do in life that I feel like I do well.

I do a lot of things mediocre, but I don't do anything, one thing, real good except for driving the race car. So [the answer is] being in the race car and being able to do what I do. Obviously winning and especially the big wins, the last-lap passes, or the final shootout. Those go back to Eldora, they go back to quarter midgets, that part is still what really drives me, to be able to do spectacular things like that and to be able to pull off some great wins.

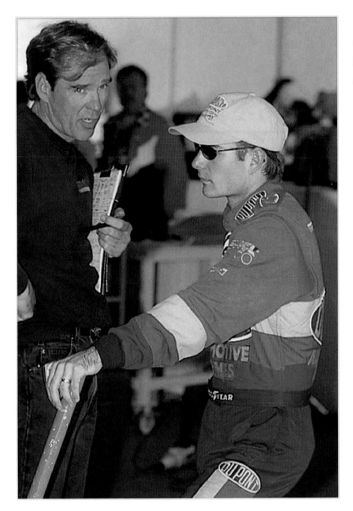

"Some days, it's very tough to get the car working just right, and Ray and I have to be one hundred percent focused and communicating." *SCR Archives*

"If you're in the garage area, I think you're here as the guest of somebody, to mingle, to see the drivers, to see the race cars, to see everything that goes on. But I don't think it is a place for you to get a bunch of autographs." *SCR Archives*

"To me it never gets boring. There's always a new challenge. It always gets tougher. It's more competitive than it's ever been." *SCR Archives*

Off the racetrack, God is important to me and Brooke is important to me. I mean, she's not only my wife, she's my best friend. We spend so much time together and we share everything. I don't know what I would do without having her in my life. I feel like if I was single right now and had the opportunities I have, I'm afraid I'd be going down the wrong path.

A lot has come together because of Brooke. My family, my parents, got me to this level and have made me the person that I am, so I'm very grateful to them. I certainly wish our relationship was a little bit closer right now. I feel like because John [Bickford] is not working for me anymore, I don't get to spend as much time with them and talk about the things we used to talk about, and that part's tough. I know it's tough on him and it's a little tough on me sometimes too. We're still friends and things are good, but they're not like they used to be.

When you think about life in general, there is such a huge gap between your life and the millions in this world who have nothing and who have no future. How is it you have been so fortunate and they haven't?

If I knew that answer I'd be a lot further along in life. I ask God that and I ask myself that, and I don't really know. I know there are people out there, younger guys than me who are more talented, that could easily step in to where I'm at with a great race car, great team, and do just as much or more. Why they don't get the opportunity I have, I don't know. I know that when it comes to racing, my parents dedicated a lot of their time to put me into good race cars.

Maybe the others didn't have the right parents or the right breaks and you did?

Definitely. And now I have God in my life and it helps me be content when I finish 30th or 35th and think that was a bad day. Now I think that wasn't a bad day. My worst day is still a great day.

It's hard to put those things in perspective and to be thinking about that because a lot of times in this business you're just thinking, "I've got to win, I've got to get a top-five, I've got to make this much money, I've got to do this, I've got to do that," and you don't think enough about the less fortunate.

That's where getting to know God and having Brooke, those things really make me more aware of how fortunate I really am.

I know one thing. You can't ask yourself that question every day because you still have to lead your life and your life still has problems. There are some days I feel like I have the greatest life and I'm very fortunate. You've got to remind yourself of those who are less fortunate, but yet you can't drag yourself down because you do lead a good life and things are going well for you.

You can't say "Why me? Why can't this happen to somebody else?" I've been dealt a deck of cards, and it's what I can do with that deck of cards that I've got to think about.

It's nice to help some people along the way with charities like the Make-A-Wish and other things that we've been able to do. I see that only getting more meaningful as I get older, especially as I have children. Those things are going to mean so much more to me, and I'll get more involved in them.

This morning a group of sick kids, some of them crippled and in wheelchairs, showed up at your truck. You came out, spent time with them, talked with them, signed things, and posed for pictures with them. I watched, and those kids—well, they were absolutely awestruck. It meant so much to them. What did it mean to you?

We're not out in the real world most of the time, we're at racetracks. To bring the real world to us really makes us think.

I'm happy if I put a smile on some kid's face and I hope it does some good for him, gets his spirits up. Who knows? It might help him fight the disease and help keep him or her alive. But at the same time, I think this might be his or her last day, so I thank God for what I have.

But then I think, "Can I do more to help those people?" It's difficult because . . . the toughest thing about my life is that everybody has something that they need. Right now I'm winning and a lot of those things are asked of me. Whether it's an interview, a picture, or if it's to see some Make-A-Wish kids, talk to Ray, drive the race car . . .

My business manager will be in here with a list of things for me to do that are all important. They'll all be things that need to be talked about. I've got my wife, my family, and friends, and they're all important. It's so hard to juggle that time and to say this is more important than that. Which thing should I do?

The toughest thing is when you've got three or four things that you think are all good things, that would mean a lot to you, and you've got to cut off one of them. I don't think a lot of people understand how difficult that can be.

But the second I sit in that race car and fire that engine up is when all that goes away, and I say, "Boy, it's all worth it."

"The whole time you're running you're thinking, 'Boy, if somebody just barely touches me or if I just barely touch the guy in front of me, he's going for a ride.' " *SCR Archives*

The guy who owns the car with this sticker is probably one of the spectators who also boos Jeff Gordon. *SCR Archives*

Every once in a while I pick up a race paper and there's a nasty letter from some race fan who says he stood around and wanted an autograph and you wouldn't give it to him. Tell those people, if you would, what it's like to be surrounded by people all the time who want autographs and to have their picture taken with you. Should the guy in the back of the line be irate because he didn't get what he wanted from you?

Autographs at the racetrack are the toughest thing for a fan to get because, number one, I'm here to drive the race car. My mind has to be very focused on that race car.

Some days, it's very tough to get the car working just right, and Ray and I have to be 100-percent focused and communicating. What a lot of people don't realize is that when I walk from the car to the truck I do the best job I can to sign as many autographs as I can, but the reason I'm going to the truck is that they've got me doing interviews, they've got me signing autographs up there in the truck for other people.

Some people don't know about the charity items or items for other crew members that we sign. I sign as many autographs as I can, but [the racetrack] is not an autograph session. I don't sit down, none of us can, and just start a line and stop at the end of that line and sign autographs for everyone.

That's what appearances are for. I like to do them so I can sign autographs. I also ask people to send in things so I can do it when it's a good time for me to bust out a whole bunch of autographs.

People don't realize how many autographs are signed. I bet I sign, it's got to be at least 100,000 autographs a year. Every weekend I'm in my motorhome and I get a stack of postcards and sign them. You sign what you can for the fans.

The worst place to get an autograph is at the racetrack. If you want an autograph, go to an autograph session or send it in. Be patient, give me some time. I never deny anybody an autograph. I always try to give somebody an autograph or a handshake or a picture. But I can't stand there and explain to everybody why I've got to go into the truck or why I've got to go to the media center or why I've got to go to the hospitality area or talk to Ray. It's really hard to explain the situation every single time.

Does being a Winston Cup race fan entitle that person to every driver's autograph at the fan's convenience?

If they get the right opportunity. If you're in the garage area, I think you're here as the guest of somebody, to mingle, to see the drivers, to see the race cars, to see everything that goes on. But I don't think it is a place for you to get a bunch of autographs. To me, it's not the place for it. I'm [at the track] to race and [help with] the car.

The crowds are booing you with a good bit of energy. You say it doesn't bother you. I can't believe it doesn't bother you to hear all those people boo.

It really doesn't. If I had my choice, sure, I'd love for them all to be cheering, but you know, if they're making noise I'm happy. I just listen for how loud it is and if it's loud then I'm happy and that's cool. There's a lot of guys out there that'll tell you being booed in this sport is a good thing because it means you're winning races, maybe too many races, that you're winning championships or too many championships. Earnhardt, after he won his seventh, I remember them booing the heck out of him.

Why do you suppose they boo?

I think it's no different than going to the Super Bowl, an NBA basketball game, or a tennis match and pulling for the underdog. The team that wins every game and the player that wins every match is the favorite and you expect him to win.

But it's kind of cool to see somebody else beat him, you know? That's the whole thing. I think there's a lot of fans out there that aren't Jeff Gordon fans, that are never going to be Jeff Gordon fans because maybe I don't fit the image that they wish to see in a driver.

I'm from California. I do things a little bit different than the way NASCAR drivers used to do it and I don't fit the stereotype of the good ol' country boy. It doesn't matter where you come from, how you dress, what kind of music you listen to, or whether you chew tobacco or not. If you're a good race car driver and you want to drive a stock car, you belong in this series.

It's not all boos. I have a lot of fans out there who do pull for me and do like the image. I've seen my fan club continue to grow. I see my Web site continue to grow. I see souvenir sales continue to grow, and that's not a number, that's not money, that just tells me that I've got a lot of fans out there. Somebody out there is cheering. I get a lot of letters that say maybe their cheers and claps aren't as loud, but they are out there cheering too, and [tell me] not to pay attention [to the booing]. You would not believe the number of letters I get that say I shouldn't pay attention to the boos. I mean, tons of letters that are saying, "That's not us."

> *"I don't think the number Earnhardt and Petty have is necessarily it.*
> *I don't look at how many records I can have before I leave this sport.*
> *Right now my goal is to win the race tomorrow."*
>
> —Jeff Gordon

But honestly, when I walk across that platform for the drivers' introduction and I hear the reaction, I just listen to it as a reaction. I don't say, "Let's see, I heard more cheers than I heard boos, so that's good." If they're making some kind of reaction, obviously I'm getting their attention, so that's good.

It's getting a little ugly, though. Are you worried about safety for you and Brooke?

I worry for Brooke. I don't worry near as much about myself.

She drove to the house the other day and I wasn't with her. I was just a few minutes behind her and there were people blocking our driveway, taking pictures, who wouldn't get out of the way to let her come in.

Those people are our fans, but they aren't the same as fans that are just interested in autographs or whatever. I don't know. That sometimes worries me. . . .

We've had a few people that just come knock on our door, drove eight hours and stuff. But the sport's growing and that's part of it. For the most part, the majority of the fans mean well. They are pleasant and kind to be around. I've had very, very few that have ever made any threats to Brooke or to me.

I've got one guy right now that's portraying me. That worries me because I don't know what he's doing and who is going to actually believe him. I know the guy and he looks identical to me: size, hair, everything. He is a fan of mine, but he's starting to portray being me and telling people he is me and signing my autograph. Who knows where that can lead? That worries me.

You've had so many great things happen to you, caused so many great things to happen. There's winning the Winston Cup championship, the Winston Million, the Southern 500, the Daytona 500, the Busch Clash, the Brickyard 400. So many wonderful things have happened to you already. What can there be to do from here?

Plenty. Plenty. After you win one championship, every year you just look for the next one.

So, is the plan to win eight championships?

I don't think the number Earnhardt and Petty have is necessarily it. I don't look at how many records I can have before I leave this sport. Right now my goal is to win the race tomorrow. Right now my goal is to win [another] championship. The number isn't going to mean anything to me until I get to six or seven, if I get to that. If I did get to that, then the number might mean something to me.

The [concept of] 200 wins means nothing to me right now, but if I got to about 150 I might start thinking about it. So right now I just think about what is the ultimate thing to accomplish in this sport. Winning races, winning the Daytona 500, the Brickyard, the Winston Million, things like that, and winning the championship. So those are the things I go after.

To me it never gets boring. There's always a new challenge. It always gets tougher. It's more competitive than it's ever been.

I amaze myself and the team amazes me.

I want to learn more about the Bible and get even closer to God, and I want to have a family some day. I want to have children in a couple of years. Brooke and I are really enjoying ourselves right now. We're having the time of our lives. We need to settle down a little more before we have children. We need at least another year or two before we feel like we're ready to start having children. And who knows, we might not be able to have children. Some drivers have had a difficult time having children. So we don't want to wait too long. But I would say if we could plan it, I'd say for it to be when Brooke and I are around 30.

Let's change gears. Talladega and Daytona are terrorizing to watch, seeing you guys run so fast, so close together. Is it as frightening in the car as it is to watch?

Well, the whole time you're running you're thinking, boy, if somebody just barely touches me or if I just barely touch the guy in front of me, they're going for a ride. The roof flaps have helped tremendously. We're seeing a lot fewer cars get airborne than we used to and I'm happy for that, but still, at those speeds, when you do lose control the wreck never ends. It just goes on and on and on.

The potential for getting hurt is much greater at a place like that. When you're running side by side and you can't pass because you've got cars on the inside of you and the wall is outside, and all of a sudden you see a guy drive down the middle, that's when you start to think, "Man, we've got to do something about this. We just can't have this."

It's great for the fans, though. It gets to where you have to start taking more risks to get to the front, and even when you get there you don't break away. It doesn't necessarily scare me or make me nervous. It just makes me worry about the potential for a big wreck when I see things like that.

I may just think about it for an extra second, when before I wouldn't even think about it. All of us want to get out there and get in the front pack, get in line and just break away, but it doesn't happen anymore. If you get four or five guys and you break away, all of a sudden—boom—here comes a pack of 20 cars that runs you down. It's pretty amazing. I know the fans like to see the big packs and the close racing. It can be real exciting and really awesome if we come out of it without a big wreck.

But sometimes it's like what happened to me at Talladega in October. I'm driving along, cut a left rear tire in front of 30 cars, and 20 of them wreck. That's not good. It's something that's out of your control, but if the pack wasn't quite so intense and so tight, that one might have only been a five-car wreck.

I'm just glad nobody got hurt.

"Stan Shoff did fire me, flat out, because I tore up too much stuff. I was wreckin' every race." *SCR Archives*

> *"So there definitely were times along the way that were not good. I look at them as just learning years, education, but some people could look at them as times that weren't real good, even though they still weren't real bad."*
>
> —Jeff Gordon

When you get out of the race car after one of these major events, a grueling 500-miler at a place like Charlotte, Talladega, or Daytona, what are you physically like? Do you lose weight?

It depends on the day. Bristol and Martinsville used to be the toughest places for me. I worked out a lot over the winter and that helped, but I can't work out as much during the season because it's so hectic.

We've worked hard on getting more fresh air to me. But it's not always comfortable. Like the Charlotte race. I changed some things in my helmet, and 30 laps into the race my head was being rubbed raw. So all day long I'm adjusting my helmet trying to keep that from happening. Then my fresh-air blower wasn't working right, so I was getting carbon monoxide. Then I got dehydrated and my lips started cracking. By the end of that race, I was really worn out, and it wasn't that hot a day.

I was just literally beat after that race, and it really worried me.

Most races I'll lose five pounds. Some races I'll lose more than that, but very seldom do I lose more than five pounds. I don't have a lot of weight to lose. I fluctuate from 145 to 150. At the start of [last year] I was about 155. I gained a lot of muscle and ate a lot, really had my weight up. [During the season] I wasn't eating as much and I would lose weight and not gain as much back. A couple of months [before the season ended] I was down to almost 140. I couldn't gain the weight back. I didn't have much of an appetite, and when I'd get in the car and sweat, everything I'd gained I'd lose right away. If I had to test for a couple of days in a week, boy, I was really shot by the time I got to the race.

So I've worked real hard on fluids and just eat as much as I can. [Last fall] Brooke and I went on vacation with some friends for six days and it was the greatest thing. We had somebody who cooked food for us every day: breakfast, lunch, and dinner. We were totally relaxed and having fun. You could be as active as you wanted to or as relaxed as you wanted. I gained probably five pounds and got back up to about 150 and I needed that. It got my appetite back to eating a whole lot too.

My schedule is so hectic, a lot of times I skip breakfast and then I won't eat lunch until 4 o'clock. I find Ray and the guys doing the same thing sometimes and it's a bad habit.

Some of the people think that because you've had so much success you've never failed at anything you've tried. Have you ever failed at something you tried hard to succeed at?

Most people who know me now know me through Winston Cup or Busch Grand National, so they are going to look pretty much at the last seven years of my life.

I'll never forget getting fired from a couple of different rides. [Sprint car owner] Gary Stanton told me, "You're a great kid and you drove the wheels off the thing, but I need more." I wouldn't say he fired me, but we mutually agreed [being together] wasn't the best thing. Maybe I wasn't ready for the World of Outlaws at the time. He'll probably deny it [laughing].

But [sprint car owner] Stan Shoff did fire me, flat out, because I tore up too much stuff. I was wreckin' every race!

I tell you what. I felt as much pressure driving that car as I did when I was a rookie in Winston Cup. Here I was in this great car, good motors, had everything you'd need to win.

We ran pretty good, never won any dirt races, but we won some pavement races. I remember we went to Sharon for an all-star race. A guy spins, I drill him, and I flip. We rebuilt the car and I went out for the next race, and I flipped again. I wrecked two cars in one night. We went to Knoxville [for the

Nationals, sprint car racing's biggest event of the year]. We were in the show, running good, and we went out for one of those Race of the States deals. Flipped a good car. Tore the race car all up and had to bring another car out.

I tore up a bunch of race cars, but I was standin' on the gas so they kept me in there. The last straw on the Stan Shoff deal was when we went to a little track near their shop. Stan's there telling his buddies, "Watch this kid, we're gonna win." He came over to me and said he needed me to win that race. It's supposed to be a cake walk because there's all these local guys, and here we come in with the big hauler and big motors, car, everything.

I go out there and I tear the thing up.

That was it. I knew that night he was going to fire me—and he did. And you know what? That was probably the best thing that ever happened to me because after that John [Bickford] and I put our own race car together. We started running the USAC pavement shows. I drove for Rollie Helmling, Bob East, and Pepsi, and boy, did things turn around. I started winning a bunch of pavement TV races on ESPN, running USAC sprint cars and midgets. The next three years were awesome, and then, boom, I found myself down here in the Busch Series.

So there definitely were times along the way that were not good. I look at them as just learning years, education, but some people could look at them as times that weren't real good, even though they still weren't real bad.

Life is very good now.

Gordon says the hecklers and their boos (and even obscene gestures) really doesn't bother him. *SCR Archives*

GORDON CAPTURES 2ND BRICKYARD WIN

BY BOB MYERS
Circle Track, December 1998

Editor's Note: Proving his first win at the fabled Indy track was no fluke, and that sometimes it pays to be lucky instead of merely good, Gordon and the No. 24 team firmly established themselves as a "money" team with this win. That is, one that when all the chips are on the table, they can step up their game to a level to clear it.

With NASCAR celebrating its golden anniversary, Jeff Gordon wants to etch his name and accomplishments so deeply in Winston Cup history and lore that he'll be remembered 50 years from now. If the youthful wonder is as successful in the next 15 or 20 years as he has been for 5, he'll rewrite the books as one of the all-time great drivers.

Gordon gave himself a present for his 27th birthday, becoming the first two-time winner of the rich and prestigious Brickyard 400 at hallowed Indianapolis Motor Speedway.

Winning the inaugural Brickyard 400 in 1994 was awesome, but the second "just blows me away," he says. "Every day just seems to get better, and I can't believe all these things are happening. I dream about things like this, but I don't really believe they will happen. And all of a sudden they do, and I don't know what to think."

When there are big bucks and prestige for grabs, Gordon comes to the table and cleans the plate. He was wowed by his motorsports-record $1,637,625 winner's prize at Indy. One million dollars was the amount of the Winston No Bull 5 bonus, claimed for the first time. The other $637,625 was from the $5.5 million purse, which paid up to 43rd, or last place, in the race.

It wasn't altogether money, exposure, and degree of difficulty that made Gordon's Brickyard victory sweet. Having resided in Pittsboro, down the road from Indianapolis, when he was racing sprint cars, Gordon is embraced by fans from Indiana and environs as their own. The multitude of 300,000 roared approvingly of Gordon's victory, drowning boos, if there were any. "After the race, when I came down pit road, I actually shut off the engine. I had to hear it. It was awesome," he says.

The start of what is now considered the second most important race in Cup racing, the Brickyard 400. *Nigel Kinrade*

Ray Evernham and Jeff Gordon celebrate their second Brickyard win in five years. *Sam Sharpe*

Gordon and the Rainbow Warriors were darn near perfect in the race. Gordon led 97 of the 160 laps and held off Mark Martin's menacing Ford to the race-ending caution. Martin puts the outcome in perspective: "He had the lead and the faster car, and that's a tough combination to beat." There was some solace for Martin in winning the first IROC race at Indy and clinching his record fourth—third straight—$225,000 IROC Series championship.

Luck was a substantial factor too, with Gordon capitalizing fortuitously on the adversity of worthy Ford opponents. Dale Jarrett, whose Robert Yates Racing Taurus was clearly the best car in the field, ran out of gas in the lead at halfway, either a potential $1.6 million—Jarrett was eligible for the No Bull prize—miscalculation or a gamble to collect a $10,000 mid-race bonus. "[It was] stupid," says crewman Steve Allen. "We figured we could go 79 laps. We got greedy and tried to run 80 laps, and didn't make it." However, car-owner Yates says the gas gaffe was an honest mistake, albeit costly. The car's powerful engine guzzled more fuel than anticipated as Jarrett built a four-second lead. That Jarrett, the 1996 Brickyard champ, made up four laps and finished 16th to stay alive in the points chase was a testimony to his car's prowess.

Despite all of the hoopla over the victory, Gordon's crew chief and best buddy Ray Evernham remains down to earth. "We didn't win the Brickyard 400," says Evernham. "A couple of Fords lost it."

The No. 88 Quality Care crew desperately push Dale Jarrett down pit road after a miscalculation in fuel mileage caused him to run out of gas. He was leading at the halfway point at the time.
Sam Sharpe

Ernie Irvan had the pole and led for 24 laps. He eventually finished sixth. *Nigel Kinrade*

A full-field pit stop provides a lot of fast action. *Nigel Kinrade*

Gordon plays press photogs like a fiddle at his historic second win at the Brickyard. *SCR Archives*

Mark Martin had to work his way from 13th to challenge Jeff Gordon after a lug nut popped off a wheel of his Roush Racing Taurus during a late pit stop.

The rear-end gear broke in Jeff Burton's strong Ford. The team Fords of Jeremy Mayfield, who crashed, and eighth-place Rusty Wallace had camber problems that wore out tires.

Third-place Bobby Labonte had a better Pontiac than last year, when he finished second on gas mileage, but he was no match for Martin and Gordon.

Mike Skinner's fourth and Dale Earnhardt's fifth indicated that owner Richard Childress' strategy to swap crew chiefs Larry McReynolds and Kevin Hamlin in June is paying dividends—a Brickyard 400 total of $356,600 in prize earnings.

Rookies Steve Park, healthy again after a March crash, and Indianapolis native Kenny Irwin, ran impressively in the top 10 until accidents intervened.

Ernie Irvan, who almost won the 400 twice with Yates Racing, shared a smattering of Gordon's joy. The veteran driver's second straight Brickyard pole and the two days of exposure it generated as well as his 24 laps in front and his solid sixth-place finish were a windfall boost to his second-year MB2 Racing Pontiac team and the sponsor, Skittles. Irvan didn't crack the top 5 in 19 races, but logged six top 10s, including three sixth-place finishes. "It's a big step in our progress," says Irvan.

LETTER FROM RICHARD PETTY

Circle Track, March 1999

Gordon: Top of the World... For Now

Nigel Kinrade

It seems a lot of race fans want to talk about Jeff Gordon these days, and that is quite normal. Jeff is the hottest thing going, and fans want to know how he has accomplished so much in such a short time.

I don't have all the answers, but I can pass on my opinion. A whole lot of it is timing. It is his time, and he is taking advantage of it. He has the best of every-thing—the best crew, the best car, just the best of everything under one roof.

Also, the kid is good. Don't ever doubt that. He has all the confidence in the world in him-self, his crew, and his car. He reminds me of Cale Yarborough and David Pearson. Jeff can ride all afternoon on 75 percent of his ability. Then, when he smells victory, he climbs up in that seat and gives 110 percent toward the finish. That makes everybody on his team look good.

Yarborough and Pearson were the same way. You'd race all afternoon and think you had them beat. Then something would happen and they'd be back in the chase. You'd think they were two different drivers

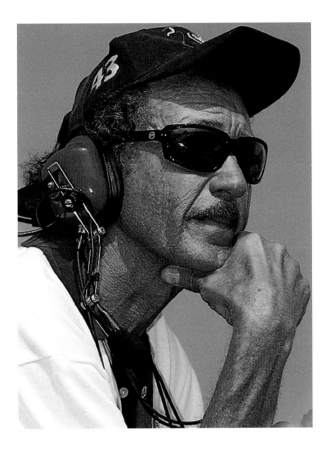

Richard Petty, the sage of stock car racing, knows every racer has a time and he places Gordon in perspective in the sport.
SCR Archives

from the way they came alive when they thought they had a pretty good chance to win. And let me point out right here that I don't believe any driver gives 100 percent all the time. In fact, I'm sure no one does.

Gordon is not the only driver who has hit the timing right and taken advantage of his day at the top.

If fans will remember, it wasn't long ago that it seemed impossible for anyone to beat Dale Earnhardt. At the height of his career, Earnhardt was unbeatable.

Bill Elliott had a few good years in the mid-1980s. It didn't seem as though anybody could beat him the year [1985] he won 11 races and the Winston Million at Darlington.

Darrell Waltrip dominated for several seasons, and so did Yarborough as did Rusty Wallace. And, yes, I had my time at the top too, despite the Pearsons, Lorenzens, and Allisons.

We were all lucky, and I believe it is destiny. I think the good Lord gives you this ability, and you better do with it what you can while you can. Let me assure you of one thing, and I don't care if your name is Gordon, Earnhardt, Yarborough, Waltrip, or whatever. It ain't going to last, buddy. Age is going to catch up with you.

So, I'll tell Gordon or anybody else. There is very little room at the top, and when you're up there, you darn well better take advantage of everything coming your way. You are not going to stay long because somebody is coming along who will clip your wings.

I laugh and tell people it is like the days of the old West. You might be the fastest gun-slinger today, last week, and maybe next week, but if you keep slapping leather long enough, one day you're gonna look up and the sun will be in your eyes. Then you're gonna get shot dead in your tracks. That's how fast it can happen in racing too.

It happens the same way in all sports. Maybe we notice it more in racing, but the New York Yankees once dominated baseball. Then that team went away for several years and now it is back on top. It's the same way with the Green Bay Packers. It dominated several years ago, then didn't have much of a team, and now it is back on top.

The biggest difference between Gordon and the rest of us is probably the publicity. When I was winning or some of the others were winning, just about the only people who kept up with it were the die-hard race fans. Now the world knows when Gordon wins a race, and that makes a big difference.

When I talk to race fans about all this, someone will ask me how long I think Gordon will dominate. I have no idea. He may have won his last race, or he may continue to win 13 races a season for the next 20 years.

That's life. That's fate, and nobody has an answer, except the man upstairs.

GORDON'S DOMINANCE: THE REALITY

OPINION BY JOHN SNYDER
Stock Car Racing, May 1999

The dominance of America's top stock car circuit by one driver is nothing new. It happens all the time.

If you'd just won $1,000,000 for the Winston No Bull at Daytona in 1999, you'd go wild too.
Nigel Kinrade

Some people think Jeff Gordon's dominance of NASCAR Winston Cup racing will be the sport's downfall. Fans writing in the weekly race papers fulminate about Gordon and his band of Rainbow Warriors, while columnists in these same papers stoke the fires of discontent with hand-wringing commentary decrying a lack of competition in NASCAR's premier division. TV's talking heads have joined in, overplaying Gordon's four-year run of 40 victories in 127 starts.

The idea that Gordon's Winston Cup success is a unique phenomenon is without merit. With few exceptions, one driver has always been top dog in NASCAR's modern era. The pinnacle of the Winston Cup mountain is small and slippery. Seldom have more than two or three drivers ever been able to cling to the top simultaneously.

Last season, Gordon won 13 of 33 races and his third Winston Cup championship. He was pursued doggedly by Mark Martin, who won seven times. Dale Jarrett was third in number of wins with three. Although 11 different drivers reached victory lane last year, no one other than Gordon, Martin, and Jarrett earned more than two trophies.

Dale Earnhardt and Richard Petty have seven Cup championships each, so Gordon still has a racing goal to work toward. *SCR Archives*

Only one man has won three Cup championships in a row, the incomparable Cale Yarborough. *SCR Archives*

Since 1972, when NASCAR reorganized the Winston Cup division, this same scenario—just three drivers posting three or more wins—has occurred 14 times. In 1987—when Dale Earnhardt won 11 times and Bill Elliott captured six checkered flags—no one else won more than twice.

As in the NFL, parity has been a NASCAR buzzword. This concept has led to the PR phrase "On Any Given Sunday." The only problem is that the numbers don't support the thesis. Using the number of drivers with three or more wins as the measure, only once has the sport achieved a semblance of parity. In 1979—with 31 events on the Winston Cup schedule—Darrell Waltrip won seven races, Richard Petty and Bobby Allison five each, Cale Yarborough four, and Buddy Baker and Neil Bonnett each won three times.

If fans tired of seeing Gordon and Martin dominate victory lane in 1998, what about 1974? That year Petty and Yarborough each won 10 races, and David Pearson crossed the line first 7 times. These three Hall of Fame drivers won 27 of the 30 races on the schedule.

Friendly enemies (ha!), drivers Bobby Allison (left) and Richard Petty, squared off against each other in another round of auto racing's keenest rivalry when the 1973 season opened. *SCR Archives*

Here's the lesson of history: More often than not, a single driver piles up wins (and money) to the (exclusion) of the other competitors. Gordon's 13 wins in 1998 matched Petty's 1975 total. In 1981 and 1982, Darrell Waltrip won 12 times. Others with big years include 11-time winners Pearson (1973), Elliott (1985), and Dale Earnhardt (1987). Registering 10 wins in a season were Allison (1972), Petty (1974), Yarborough (1974 and 1978), Pearson (1976), Rusty Wallace (1993), and Gordon (1997 and 1996). Winning lots of races is nothing new.

When Petty won 13 times in 1975, Buddy Baker was second with just four victories, creating the greatest discrepancy between the top two winners in modern Winston Cup history. Other years with big spreads between the top winner and the next guy were 1985, when Elliott bested Earnhardt 11 wins to 4, and 1982 with Waltrip's 12-to-5 margin over Allison.

Interestingly, the number of different winners each year has fallen within a relatively close range. The big exception was 1974, when only five different drivers tasted champagne. At the other end of the spectrum—in 1988, 1990, and 1991—there were 14 different winners. Eleven different drivers have won races in each of the past four years, a number slightly higher than the modern-era average of 10. These figures provide objective evidence that parity may actually be increasing.

In Winston Cup, the more things change, the more they remain the same. Throughout the 27-year history of the modern series, one or two drivers have dominated each season. Jeff Gordon, as spectacular as he has been the past four years, is only carrying on a tradition begun more than a quarter century ago by Petty, Pearson, and Allison; continued by Yarborough and Waltrip; and upheld more recently by Earnhardt, Elliott, and Wallace.

DOMINATOR OF THE DECADE

BY JON FITZSIMMONS AND STEVE ZEPEZAUER
Circle Track, December 1999

Dale Earnhardt vs. Jeff Gordon: Who is the Driver of the 1990s?

When it comes to people who dominated NASCAR Winston Cup racing
in the 1990s, Dale Earnhardt and Jeff Gordon
are the championship dominators. Earnhardt
has claimed four championships while
Gordon claimed three (so far). The only other
people to squeak in a championship during
the 1990s were Terry Labonte in 1996 and
the late Alan Kulwicki in 1992. Numerous
showdowns on the track speak volumes
about Gordon and Earnhardt, perhaps the
most memorable being the 1999 Daytona
500, where Earnhardt left a subtle reminder
in the form of tire mark donuts on Gordon's
car following the checkers.

While the topic remains infinitely debat-
able, the fact remains that the line is blurry in
regards to who was the dominant force of the
1990s. Some people say Earnhardt; others
say Gordon. We say . . .

SCR Archives

Nigel Kinrade

Statistically, one could argue that Earnhardt earned the reputation as Dominator of the
Decade—four championships in one decade compared to Gordon's three (as of deadline for
this issue, Dale Jarrett is the heavy favorite to win the 1999 title). Statistically though, Gordon
has won more races, has a higher average point standing (albeit it includes three fewer years
of racing in the 1990s than Earnhardt), and has won more money. The winnings aspect can
be discounted to some degree, considering the purses are bigger in 1999 than in 1990.

Gordon's 2.8 average in the final point standings and the 46 wins (up to the 1999
Brickyard 400) can't be denied. Neither can the fact that Gordon has won two Brickyard
400s and two Daytona 500s in the decade. Earnhardt supporters can point to the
Intimidator's total dominance in the first half of the 1990s, including four championships
in five years. Regardless of what side of the Earnhardt/Gordon fence you're on, there's
enough fodder to keep the debate going for decades to come.

THE INTIMIDATOR
VS. THE WONDER BOY

Dale Earnhardt's Results 1990–1999

Year	Races	Wins	Total Money Won	Point Standing
1990	29	9	$3,083,056	1st
1991	29	4	$2,396,685	1st
1992	29	1	$915,463	12th
1993	30	6	$3,353,789	1st
1994	31	4	$3,300,733	1st
1995	31	5	$3,154,241	2nd
1996	31	2	$2,285,926	4th
1997	32	0	$2,151,909	5th
1998	33	1	$2,990,749	8th
1999	20/34*	1*	$1,883,749*	7th*
totals	315	33	$25,516,300	4.2 (average)

Jeff Gordon's Results 1992–1999

Year	Races	Wins	Total Money Won	Point Standing
1993	30	0	$765,168	4th
1994	31	2	$1,779,523	8th
1995	31	7	$4,347,343	1st
1996	31	10	$3,428,485	2nd
1997	32	10	$6,375,658	1st
1998	33	13	$9,306,584	1st
1999	20/34*	4*	$4,179,241*	6th*
totals	208	46	$30,182,002	3.3 (average)

* Not a final result. Race 20 was the Brickyard 400 on August 7.

BRIAN WHITESELL

A NASCAR Winston Cup Rising Star

BY BOB MYERS
Circle Track, April 2000

Brian Whitesell was a surprise pick to be elevated to crew chief for Gordon when Ray Evernham left to form his own team.
Sam Sharpe

When Ray Evernham, the only crew chief Jeff Gordon had known in a meteoric rise to NASCAR Winston Cup's summit over seven years, left Hendrick Motorsports last September, competitors and observers were sure that the sport's standard-bearing No. 24 team would struggle or fall apart.

But Brian Whitesell, apparently Hendrick Motorsports' best-kept secret, a virtual unknown outside the organization and Winston Cup garage, stepped out of the shadows and into his former mentor's position as the sport's most visible—perhaps enviable—crew chief.

Though Whitesell had no name and no experience as a crew chief, the 35-year-old small-town Virginian was the logical choice for the job, hand-picked by Evernham and Gordon and readily approved by owner Rick Hendrick and company President John Hendrick. Whitesell has been with the team since its inception in 1992, through 49 victories and three championships.

As protégé of Evernham, Whitesell had learned all the aspects of how to make a stock car go fast, rising from hauler-driver to team engineer. He had been at Evernham's side, just out of camera and interview range, doing everything but sitting on the war wagon calling the shots. "I knew the basics of automotive engineering but not the basics of race cars," says Whitesell, a mechanical engineering graduate of Virginia Tech. "Working with Ray helped me understand the dynamics involved between driver, crew chief, and spotter on race days. Jeff and I have always communicated very well."

Still, Whitesell wasn't sure he'd get the job and wasn't convinced he wanted it. At least one candidate for crew chief turned down Hendrick's overture, creating a misconception. If Hendrick had hired an outsider to replace Evernham, Whitesell would have become the No. 24 team's general manager.

The Beat Went On

The Warriors didn't miss a beat, however. Whitesell promptly led Gordon to victory in his first race in command, at Martinsville, calmly making the decisive call. Team members hoisted the rookie on their shoulders, and Gordon sprayed him with champagne—not the usual Winston Cup baptism. Whitesell and the irrepressible team duplicated the feat in his second race, at Charlotte. Old-timers scratched their noggins trying to remember if a Winston Cup crew chief had won his first race, much less his first two. "I think I should retire now while I'm on top . . . The only way I can go is down," Whitesell dryly joked after the Charlotte victory.

"I don't want to see Brian talking to anybody about a job," interjected Rick Hendrick."

More importantly, the victories, especially at Martinsville, were likely the most significant in the team's illustrious history, answering a lot of questions regarding the team's solidarity, refuse-to-lose attitude and chemistry, and Whitesell's acceptance and ability. Moreover, the wins proved quite conclusively that no one person—not even Evernham—holds the key to No. 24's success. It could not have gotten any better at the time.

Whitesell would have been happy with top-10 finishes until he got his feet firmly on the ground. "I just didn't want our performance to fall off," he says. "Unless something adverse happened, we were almost always a top-five car with Ray. I figured that if I could keep us in the top ten for a few races while we worked out the bugs, we could win a race by the end of the season. To win our first two races was unreal." However, reality reappeared with a 12th at Talladega, after Gordon led the most laps, and an 11th at Rockingham.

"There had been real concerns about how the team would respond," adds Whitesell, "because of all the controversy that surrounded Ray's departure. People felt the distractions would ruin the team and that it was washed up. I tried to make sure the guys realized that we could carry on as we were, but it seemed hard to convince them when Ray had been such an emotional leader and such a big part of the team for so long."

Brian Whitesell's meteoric rise in Winston Cup racing now includes two wins as crew chief for Jeff Gordon with the No. 24 DuPont team.
Nigel Kinrade

"Ray had told us," Whitesell continues, "that if he, in his words, 'ever got hit by a bus,' we could still win. That was the point I tried to make, as crew chief, the first time I talked with the guys. I told them Ray wasn't going to be here but that he had taught and trained us how to do this without him. I added that if we do not succeed without him, it would be a big letdown to him and everybody in our circle. We knew what we had to do, and we just did it. It's not Jeff Gordon or me; it's the group, and that's what I'm most proud of."

Whitesell says he is not an Evernham and doesn't pretend to be. "We're different," Whitesell says.

Keeping the Chemistry

"I was the one who pushed very hard for Brian," Gordon says, "because I wanted to keep that team chemistry we've always had. Brian is very intelligent, and he's learned from the best, Ray. He knows how our guys work, knows their likes and dislikes. . . . We have a good relationship. Now we're working closer together, and things couldn't be better [as of late October 1999]. He's already proved himself. I feel like when he gets more experience, he's very capable of becoming the best crew chief in the garage. Also, it was good to see Brian move up. It gave our guys strength and encouragement that people can advance in the organization. Look where Brian started with the No. 24 team and where he is now. I think the guys have rallied around him and myself to make this team even stronger."

Now that Whitesell has races and wins behind him, the quest for a fourth championship seems more realistic in 2000. The team was knocked out of title contention in 1999 by at least six DNFs that resulted in finishes of 32nd and below. "We've had a lot of bad luck that we haven't had in the past," Whitesell says, "but we still have the most wins and the most poles [7 of each through 30 races in 1999]. The performance is still there. Our season is comparable to others we've had. This team has been as strong as it ever was, and I think the two wins back to back substantiated that."

Not a Pretender

Whitesell says he is not an Evernham and doesn't pretend to be. "We're different," Whitesell says. "Ray has always been a racer [a former modified driver]. He learned everything hands-on and has common sense. For five years, all I did was study racing; I didn't try to figure out why something worked. Now I'm able to apply engineering to racing.

"Ray had developed into a leader and a coach. He is very aggressive and motivated. I am very motivated but not aggressive. I try to look at and understand something, and make decisions based on the engineering side rather than the racing side.

"I want to get ideas from my people and try to establish open communication. I want their feedback. I'm still going to make decisions based on the whole picture, all of which some of the guys may not see. Ray had an all-encompassing knowledge. He knew practically everyone's job in the shop. I don't and don't claim to, so I'm using the guys more for feedback. Ray didn't have to rely on that; he was able to make his own decisions. No one can do this by himself. I just want to keep my guys happy. Happy people do a good job."

Whitesell, 5 feet 7 inches and 160 pounds, is laid-back and low-key, the antithesis of Evernham: calculating, deliberate, and meticulous—a perfectionist with a slide-rule approach. "I'm certainly not hyperactive," he says. "I've got a little southern boy from Virginia in me, and I do things at a slower pace and more deliberately. I have enough good people around me to keep me fired up. I've always been accused of being a bit too precise and perfect with anything I do. That has its good and bad points. I try to learn from my mistakes rather than keep making the same mistakes." Whitesell, who

kept all of the No. 24 team's records, keeps a notepad and pen handy, including during this interview, "in case something pops into my head that I need to write down."

Most of the early changes Whitesell made were of necessity. When Evernham received a provisional release from his Hendrick contract, which ran through 2006, to become a team owner and lead the return of DaimlerChrysler's Dodge Division to Winston Cup in 2001, he took with him chief mechanic Ed Guzzo and two other crewmen. That was approved in his release. Evernham also offered Whitesell a job.

Rising to the Challenge

To cover the losses, Whitesell broke up responsibilities and assigned two people to each vacant position. "Tony Gibson, who was Bill Elliott's crew chief for a short time, and Steve Letarte have picked up Ed's duties at the shop and track," Whitesell says. "I've taken some of Ray's responsibilities with Mark Thoreson and Pete Haferman. Darren Mariska has my former duties. Bootie Barker is doing a lot of shock work. But all the policies and procedures are the same. These guys have done an outstanding job."

And Gordon, now a part owner of the team after signing a lifetime contract with Rick Hendrick, has become more involved. "Jeff is a lot more interested in what's under his car, what springs, shocks, sway bar," Whitesell says. "Before, Jeff drove the car, gave Ray input, and Ray made all of the decisions. Now Jeff is helping make the calls on what needs to be changed on the car and what areas we need to work on.

"Jeff is certainly the team leader now. Obviously from the results, he is a big part. But he can't win when parts break or things fall off his car. He will take the car to victory lane if he has the opportunity. It's up to us to give him that opportunity. I think there are some excellent drivers in Winston Cup who do not have the opportunity to win because of circumstances that take them out of contention. On the other hand, Jeff is so good that it helps us keep key people together here because they know their efforts are going to be rewarded."

Ready for Racing

Whitesell says he's comfortable—"no butterflies"—making the calls on race day and, having been close to Gordon and Evernham, he is familiar with the faces and cameras of the media. The difference is that the focus is on him. "I never felt I had to be a part of the limelight," Whitesell says, "and that's one reason I got along so well with Ray and Jeff. Ed (Guzzo) and I were content to work behind the scenes. I've always been like that." The hardest part of the transition, he says, is that in addition to focusing on the car, he has to manage the 35-member team, including the pit crew and the shop.

Whitesell has worked his way from the bottom to the top in racing with persistence and determination. Growing up in native Stuart Drafts, a town of about 5,000 in Virginia's Shenandoah Valley, Whitesell

Brian Whitesell's original contributions to the No. 24 came behind the scenes as an ace chassis tech man. *SCR Archives*

Opposite: Jeff Gordon's No. 24 DuPont team will be led by Brian Whitesell as team manager and Robbie Loomis as crew chief in 2000. *Harold Hinson*

became interested in things mechanical through his father, who worked as a mechanic at DuPont—coincidentally and ironically the No. 24 team's primary sponsor—and repaired small engines as a sideline.

Whitesell, his interest sparked, began working on his personal vehicle, a Jeep CJ-5, and the souped-up Novas, Chevelles, and Camaros of his high school friends. "I spent more time working on cars than I did socializing or anything else," he says. Whitesell had considered studying architecture in college, but his interest in automobiles prevailed and took him to Virginia Tech (VTI). While there, Whitesell designed, from the tires up, a mini-Baja four-wheel drive, all-terrain vehicle powered by a Briggs and Stratton engine, for an annual racing competition conducted by the Society of Automotive Engineers among East Coast colleges. "The car didn't do too well," Whitesell recalls, "and it was a lesson on how to get prepared in advance. We ran everything up to the deadline, and the vehicle wasn't tested. But I knew at that point I wanted to race for a living and to become a crew chief."

Through VTI's co-op program, Whitesell worked at the Volvo White plant, where tractors for 18-wheelers are built, in Dublin, Virginia. That experience helped pay his way through school and led to a job as test engineer with Mack trucks in Allentown, Pennsylvania, after he received his degree. When the trucks went into production in Winnsboro, South Carolina, Whitesell helped with the startup program, which led to a full-time position.

While at Winnsboro, Whitesell started going to Charlotte in search of a race team he could help voluntarily. "I got in touch with [the late] Alan Kulwicki," Whitesell says. "He was going through hard times with sponsors, and I figured he could use the help. I considered that a good place to start. I worked my regular job and traveled to the races on the weekends, doing odd jobs. Because I did not know anyone and had no ins in the sport, I had to do it all, just to prove how dedicated I was. I was willing to do the dirty work with the hope of having a glory job down the road." There he met Ray Evernham, then a Kulwicki mechanic.

Answering the Call

When Evernham signed with Hendrick to establish the No. 24 team and lead Gordon, Whitesell followed and became the truck driver, the only job available. He deemed that as his best opportunity to work full time—and get paid—in racing. In two years, he advanced to the newly created position of team engineer and later to supervisor of five Hendrick engineers. He was named Western Auto's Winston Cup mechanic of the year in 1997. But his goal as crew chief was met much quicker than he expected.

Whitesell and his wife Mary have been married for two years. They were introduced two years earlier by former Hendrick crew chief Phil Hammer. She has worked as an assistant to ASA driver Mike Miller and in racing for most of her life. "We have a lot of mutual goals," says Whitesell. "Eventually, she wants to be part of our team." When there's leisure time, they enjoy working in their yard. Whitesell also likes to hunt on a spread he owns in the Virginia mountains, but hasn't done so in two years. He fancies his wife's Mexican dishes and favors country and rock music. "I like my music," he says. "I keep the CDs playing in my truck—and on my computer—to keep me going."

Where Whitesell is going seems to be clear; after ending the 1999 season with two wins, he has ascended to the position of team manager and intends to lead the team and new crew chief Robbie Loomis to another Winston Cup championship. But wherever the path takes him, he says, "I want to be in racing the rest of my life."

BOTH ENDS OF THE RAINBOW

BY BRUCE MARTIN
Stock Car Racing, August 2000

Jeff Gordon's Career through the Latest Ups and Downs

Just a little over one year ago, Jeff Gordon appeared to be unstoppable. At 27, he had won three NASCAR Winston Cup titles and a record-tying 13 races in one season. With Ray Evernham as his crew chief, Gordon had never gone longer than 12 races without a victory since he scored his first career win in the 1994 Coca-Cola 600 at Charlotte Motor Speedway.

Gordon had it all, and it appeared there was little his NASCAR Winston Cup competitors could do to derail him from becoming perhaps the greatest driver in Winston Cup history. But the winning combination can fall apart very quickly. Evernham was ready for a new challenge. Even

Gordon sits patiently awaiting the start of the next event. His patience would serve him well in his quest for the next victory. *Sam Sharpe*

though he wanted to wait until the end of the season to leave Hendrick Motorsports and Jeff Gordon, the distraction of the announcement was so great Evernham resigned in September 1999. He left to spearhead Daimler–Chrysler's return to the sport with the Dodge Intrepid in 2001.

A key question loomed. Was Gordon a great driver, or did Evernham make him a great driver?

Gordon quickly proved himself by winning at Martinsville and Charlotte last fall—his first two races without Evernham—with Brian Whitesell as the new crew chief.

There was turmoil on the horizon, however. When five members of the famed "Rainbow Warriors" (the over-the-wall pit crew) decided to leave Hendrick and join Robert Yates Racing to work with 1999 Winston Cup champion Dale Jarrett, Gordon's team once again faced adversity.

Despite seven wins and a fourth-place finish in the Winston Cup standings, Gordon's 1999 season paled in comparison to 1998 when he won a record-tying 13 races, his third Winston Cup title, and collected nearly $10 million in season earnings.

At the end of the 1999 season, Whitesell was elevated to team manager and Robbie Loomis was lured away from Petty Enterprises, where he had worked with drivers like Bobby Hamilton and

(above) The season opened with great promise as Hendrick Motorsports unveiled its 200 entries for Gordon, Jerry Nadeau, and Terry Labonte in January. *Harold Hinson*

(left) *SCR Archives*

Gordon experienced tough sledding in the early part of the 2000 season. The crews had to contend with body damage from race events and found it difficult to stay in the hunt. *SCR Archives*

John Andretti, to become Gordon's crew chief. The combination appeared ready to be contenders, and they had high hopes for entering the season-opening Daytona 500.

Those hopes quickly faded when Gordon finished 34th at Daytona, then 28th at Las Vegas.

Had the wonderment left the driver known as "Wonder Boy"? Even his competitors couldn't help but admit they were puzzled.

On a rainy day in March at Atlanta Motor Speedway, Gordon stood in the back of the team's transporter and exhibited confidence.

"It stands at three races, which is not a lot of races," Gordon said at the time. "We still have thirty races to go. I don't pay attention to last year. That is over and done with. At Daytona, we had a top-ten car and had something break. At Rockingham, we were in the top five for a while and we faded at the end when we got loose and finished tenth. At Las Vegas, we just missed the setup. I look at that weekend being our only really bad race for this."

Gordon continues to draw support from his legion of fans, but the media is keeping a close eye on him.

"It's like, 'Wow, we didn't expect him to win, but we didn't expect this,'" Gordon says. "That was after just three races. I knew we were going to improve every weekend and get better and it was going to take some time. We are the ones who have to be patient because everyone around us is being patient. Wow—we're human after all."

Gordon believes part of his fade was due to the ongoing development of the 2000 Chevrolet Monte Carlo, but, realistically, he knew there would be stretches in his career wherein he wouldn't be on top.

"You have to work real hard, not take anything for granted, keep the morale good, try to make the cars better, and focus more on your driving," Gordon says. "I really think the new car threw us more than anything else. I really thought this car would be better balanced than it really is at the beginning of the season."

Gordon remains excited about how his team was structured and never panicked. "It has gone very well, we just haven't been able to show it on the racetrack," Gordon says. "Robbie Loomis is pretty organized and Brian Whitesell is very organized, so those two guys make a good team. I hate that we have not run better, but we are capable of doing a lot better."

Expectation has become Gordon's greatest foe. "Everybody thinks I was just born and all of a sudden, I've gone to victory lane and have just won championships," Gordon says. "That is not true at all. This is the most competitive, toughest series there is in the world, as far as I'm concerned. I've been under the microscope. Plus, we've had so much success that if we don't continue that—you'll never be able to continue that. Who knows? We might have a year where we are off. But I'll bet you this team is not done winning championships. When you have the shakeup that we had in our team, you have to rebuild and get it back to where it needs to be. It might not happen overnight. It might take some time."

Gordon began to see signs of improvement when he won the pole for the Mall.com 400 at Darlington Raceway in March. He climbed from 24th in the Winston Cup point standings to seventh by mid-April.

But it wasn't until the victory in the DieHard 500 at Talladega Superspeedway on April 16 that he proved he's still one of the best drivers in the sport. In the closing laps of the race, Gordon did everything he could to keep Mike Skinner behind him, even driving him to the grass in an effort to block Skinner on the backstretch on the white flag lap.

It worked. Gordon won the race—the 50th win in his brief NASCAR Winston Cup career. "I couldn't be more excited," Gordon said at the time. "It's been an interesting year for us. I never lost faith in this team. I'm proud of them that they were able to overcome a lot of criticism and keep their heads up and work hard and do what it takes to win. I'm a little shocked that our first win with me and Robbie together

came here at Talladega. We weren't very fast when we tested, but in the draft, the car was just spectacular. Sometimes a car will come to life like that in the draft. I still didn't think coming from 36th that we could do what we did today. It was a great day for us."

Loomis was equally emotional, and relieved. "We've been through a lot," he admitted. "I remember when we won Phoenix with Petty Enterprises and driver Bobby Hamilton, Kyle Petty told me I'd never feel that feeling again. I've got to tell you, this feeling today felt just like that first one for me. Brian Whitesell and all of the guys put together a great pit crew, and I'm just fortunate to be in this situation."

Loomis relishes the opportunity to work with Gordon. He's worked for, arguably, two of the five greatest drivers in NASCAR history—Richard Petty as an owner and Gordon as a driver.

"That's the greatest feeling in the world," Loomis says. "Richard always told me, 'What you need is a twenty-five-year-old Richard Petty.' When I told him I was going to work with Jeff Gordon, he said I was getting pretty close.

"The way I look at it, I'm going to school right now. But you never know what happens in life. This deal came up and I made the decision to do it. You look around at all the resources they have and to work with Brian in a situation he already has organized, it's great to work with a team that has won championships."

Gordon remained a popular attraction for the media and fans throughout the team's redefining moments. *Harold Hinson/SCR Archives*

Gordon and the team felt the vindication of their struggles with the win in the DieHard 500 at Talladega Superspeedway in April. The latest version of the touted Rainbow Warrior crew gained momentum and confidence as the 2000 season rolled along. *Sam Sharpe*

For Loomis, working with Gordon is similar to getting to coach Michael Jordan.

"A three-time Winston Cup champion at twenty-eight years old, still in his prime, that's any crew chief's dream," Loomis says. "He likes knowing he is the best. There is a lot of pressure there, but pressure is another word for challenge. That's how I feel about this season—it's just a different challenge."

In the past, Gordon was one of four drivers who—for the most part—won all the races on any given week. By contrast, he was the ninth different winner in the first nine races to open the 2000 Winston Cup season.

"This whole season has been tough to win because there are so many guys capable of winning," Gordon says. "We certainly haven't been as strong as we hoped to be, and we missed a few things with the Monte Carlo. We went through some changes, but like I said, we never lost faith. This whole team, I could just see them gel a little bit better each week."

So at 28 years old, Gordon had reached yet another milestone in his fabulous career by winning 50 races, made more satisfying by overcoming a season's worth of adversity.

"That I've won 50 races and this team has won 50 races, it's a privilege," Gordon says. "As hard as it seems like I fought to win this one, it's hard for me to believe I've done that 49 other times. That's what it takes. It takes the whole deal. It's got to be your day, and today was our day.

"We hope some more of those come our way."

Crew chief Robbie Loomis keeps an eye on the activity from atop the No. 24 war wagon. *Sam Sharpe*

EFF GORDON'S
INISHES

	1999	
Daytona	1
Rockingham	39
Las Vegas	3
Atlanta	1
Darlington	3
Texas	43
Bristol	6
Martinsville	3
Talladega	38
California	1
Richmond	31
Charlotte	39
Dover	2
Michigan	2
Pocono	2
Sears Point	1
Daytona	21
New Hampshire	3
Pocono	32
Indianapolis	3
Watkins Glen	1
Michigan	2
Bristol	4
Darlington	13
Richmond	40
New Hampshire	5
Dover	17
Martinsville*	1
Charlotte	1
Talladega	12
Rockingham	11
Phoenix	10
Homestead	10
Atlanta	38

	2000	
Daytona	34
Rockingham	10
Las Vegas	28
Atlanta	9
Darlington	8
Bristol	8
Texas	25
Martinsville	4
Talladega	1

*- Brian Whitesell becomes crew chief
\#- Robbie Loomis becomes crew chief,
Brian Whitesell becomes team manager

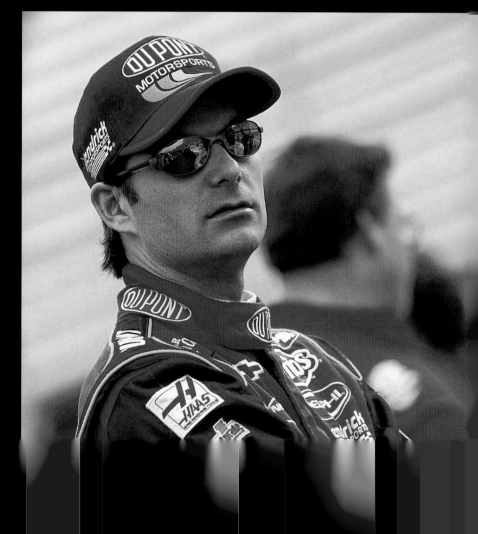

TARGET PRACTICE

BY LARRY COTHREN
Stock Car Racing, October 2001

What Makes Jeff Gordon the Most Envied and Reviled Man on the Racetrack

Ask Jeff Gordon what it's like to be the man to beat in NASCAR, the guy seemingly every other driver is aiming for, and he'll probably tell you it's just racin'.

When Tony Stewart spins Gordon out on pit road at Bristol after the March race?

Just racin'.

When Gordon has a heated confrontation on pit road with Rusty Wallace after the spring race at Richmond? Just racin'.

How about when Stewart says Gordon is the one driver he likes to beat more than any other because he's so squeaky clean? Just racin', of course.

"I have fun with that," Gordon says. "Really, it's part of the entertainment of our sport. Our sport, it's racing, but it's also entertainment. I get a chuckle out of it. Rusty and I laughed after the deal in Richmond, and Tony and I, we've talked since (the Bristol spin). It's not as big a deal as the media and the fans want to make out of it. You just go on about your job. It's racing, and you've got to race those guys every weekend."

Yes, in this homogenized new world of NASCAR, when a little verbal spin for the sake of public relations takes precedence over the reality of a situation, "Jeffspeak" is alive and well.

What, though, makes Gordon such a target for heated emotion and, sometimes, controversy? From spectators who vehemently boo and root against him to competitors who confront him or spin his car out on pit road, what gives?

Gordon is, after all, a mild mannered, relatively soft-spoken young man, nearly always polite, gracious in victory lane, seemingly respectful toward his peers, never prone to exaggerated emotion or theatrics.

Could it be, then, that Jeff Gordon, gentleman racer, is just too perfect? Indeed, too squeaky clean?

SCR Archives

A Prelude

Let's turn back the clock a few decades. In the early 1970s a brash, cocky, outgoing, young gun of a racer burst onto the NASCAR scene. A decade later he had the stock car racing world by the tail.

In 1981 and 1982, while driving for Junior Johnson, Darrell Waltrip earned consecutive Winston Cup championships. He won 12 of 31 races in 1981 and 12 of 30 races (40 percent) the next year. For a six-year period ending in 1986, when Waltrip and Johnson parted, their pairing produced 43 wins and 3 Winston Cup titles, the last one in 1985.

But Darrell Waltrip didn't just win races—he talked, he joked, he took verbal jabs at his fellow competitors, he even bragged about winning. He was so talkative, in fact, that Cale Yarborough tabbed him with the moniker "Jaws."

The name fit all too well. Waltrip relished being the man in the bull's-eye, the man stirring things up among NASCAR's old guard. The nickname wasn't merely a reference to a big-mouthed driver; it was, for all intents and purposes, a reference to the way Waltrip rocked the NASCAR boat and devoured everything in his path.

"I raised the bar back in the 1980s to a new level and fans didn't like that," says Waltrip, now a commentator for NASCAR races on FOX. "I was beating their heroes, and I was the guy who looked like I had it all. I had a beautiful wife. I was winning lots of races and championships, making a lot of money. I represented something to a lot of people that they could never achieve. That created a controversy. And in my case—I've said this time and again—I put fuel on that fire. I played with that as if it were a game. If people booed me, I'd make them madder. That was just how I was."

"He looks like he could be a star in a movie," Darrell Waltrip says. "There's so many things about him that people are so envious of, and envy is the problem in our sport." *Sam Sharpe*

No DW Here

What, then, makes Gordon susceptible to the same negative and often emotional responses from spectators and competitors? He is, after all, the very antithesis of Darrell Waltrip. Nonconfrontational. Mostly unemotional. Politically correct in speech and manner. Able to maintain an even keel in good times or bad.

Even his crew chief, Robbie Loomis, shakes his head sometimes and wonders how Jeff Gordon can still be Jeff Gordon in most any circumstance.

"From the competition-side, people wonder what is his makeup," Loomis says. "I'll be honest with you, and I work with him, but the guy is so special as far as the way he treats people and the way he handles himself even in bad times, you sit there and ask yourself, 'Man, is this guy human?' You can definitely tell

After all he's accomplished, Gordon still brings laser-like focus to the track. *SCR Archives*

Those in the garage area knew it was only a matter of time before Jeff Gordon rediscovered the winning ways that carried him to three Winston Cup championships. *Harold Hinson*

Jarrett looks at the 24 team and sees Gordon's re-emergence as nothing unusual.

"I can't say that I'm surprised because someone like Jeff Gordon, who has the kind of talent he does, and the resources Hendrick Motorsports has, you know that they're not going to struggle," says Jarrett. "He struggled to win four or five races or something like that (in 2000). That's really struggling (he says with a laugh), but you know they're not going to be behind very long. Robbie Loomis is very capable and he has a lot of good people around him, plus Jeff Gordon is a great talent. He's going to definitely be the one we battle all year, and we're going to do our best to try to keep up and keep him in sight."

Staying Focused

Winning and being back on top brings consequences, of course, even consequences you can joke about.

"I told Jeff, 'Man, all these years I built relationships for these people to like me and now all of a sudden they're not liking me,' " Loomis says with a laugh. "But we were kidding about that. It's been great. The biggest thing is probably the happy surprise it's been with his personality. He's such a thankful person. At the end of the day when we win, we look at each other and we're both very thankful for the team that we get to work with and for all the tools and stuff that Rick Hendrick supplies us with, which makes it so much easier.

"That's the thing about him that's so fun to work with him—it's not like he beats his chest and says 'I'm the best, I whupped them today.' He's just very thankful for what he does get, and sometimes he looks at it and says, 'How does all this happen?' "

When it does happen, Loomis gets to experience a situation where he and his teammates are not the most highly thought of team around the racetrack, sometimes thrust into circumstances where thick skin may be the most valuable tool a team member can have.

"We talk about it a little bit during our meetings sometimes," says Loomis. "We really have to keep the focus on our job, our cars, and what we're doing. There's going to be a lot of things from the outside that will try to distract you from that, but I think as long as we stay focused, we communicate well together, then we'll be fine."

So Loomis, having been on the outside looking in and now being an insider, may be the most qualified to answer the overriding question: Why is Gordon such a target for ill will from competitors and spectators?

"You know, I thought about that a lot before I took the job," Loomis says. "I think the biggest thing I came to when I looked at it is I was like, 'What is it that everybody doesn't like about him?' And, you know, he's a winner. If you look at anybody else, nobody likes to see a guy win all the time."

Waltrip carries the point further.

"It's real simple," he says. "When you represent perfection, when you are the perfect guy, that rubs people the wrong way. Not only that, when you have a standard as high as his is, if you do make any kind of an error, then people really want to jump on you and criticize you or boo you or whatever."

The "whatevers" have been hurled at Gordon with a fair amount of frequency in recent seasons—like when Mike Skinner won a 1997 NASCAR exhibition race in Japan and a television audience was privy to Skinner's comment to his teammates, via his headset, about beating the "little S.O.B.," or when Tony Stewart referred to Gordon as "Prince Charming" after Stewart won this summer at Sears Point.

Stewart, however—despite his remarks and aggressive action toward Gordon—downplays any notion of a rivalry between the two.

"I think the so-called rivalry between me and Jeff Gordon is overplayed," Stewart says. "I want to beat everybody week-in and week-out, and that includes Jeff."

Part of what sparked other driver's dislike of Gordon was that he had a beautiful wife. But in 2002, Brooke filed for divorce, creating more off-the-track distraction for Jeff. *SCR Archives*

Unlike Gordon, who rarely says anything that might hint of a detour from putting forth a positive PR image, Stewart is known as a driver who speaks his mind, sometimes too much, he admits. But Stewart will agree straight up that most drivers are too PR conscious, too afraid to really speak their minds.

"Absolutely. I've always thought that," Stewart says. "I feel if someone asks me an honest question, then they deserve an honest answer. That's probably why I've gotten in trouble as often as I have. People ask questions that they sometimes don't like the answers to. You'll have that."

Why, then, does Gordon—the very personification of a clean-cut, easygoing nice guy—draw so much ill will from spectators and competitors?

"I have no idea," Stewart says. "He seems to do everything right, so I don't know why he gets booed."

Just a Little Noise

There's a NASCAR adage that says it's better for a driver to hear something—anything at all—over dead silence.

"It's all about noise, man," Waltrip says. "I ain't out there counting which ones are doing what. I'm just out there listening to the noise. There's nothing any more disheartening and makes you feel any worse than to have them call out your name and you walk across that stage and nobody ever claps their hands or even acts like they know you're there. That's the kiss of death. I'm always listening. Tony Stewart gets a reaction. Jeff Gordon gets a reaction. I like the guys who get a reaction."

Waltrip, though, had an epiphany of sorts during the waning years of his heyday.

"There was a point when I had accomplished so much and I had done so much that I didn't want to hear those boos any more," says Waltrip. "It took a real effort on my part. I had to change a lot of things, had to change the way I did a lot of things to stop those boos and turn them to cheers. I had to not be the bad guy anymore; I had to become one of the good guys. It paid off for me. I was the most popular driver (as voted by fans) in 1989 and 1990. Those two awards are probably as dear to me as anything I've done—considering the fact I was so unpopular for so long."

Gordon, on the other hand, as Stewart points out "seems to do everything right." He is, seemingly, the quintessential good guy.

"He's not the kind of guy who goes out looking for controversy," Waltrip says. "He's not the kind of guy who says things that's going to create controversy. What's wrong with Jeff Gordon? The answer to that is nothing. And that's where the problem is."

STICK IT TO 'EM

- Gordon's points title at age 24, in 1995, made him the youngest champion in the sport's modern era.

- In 275 career starts (through Chicago), Gordon had finished in the Top 5 a phenomenal 140 times, or 50.9 percent of the time, and he had 177 Top 10s, for a percentage of 64.3.

- Gordon's 10 wins in 1996, 10 in 1997, and 13 in 1998, mark the first time in the sport's modern era that a driver has posted three consecutive seasons of double-digit victories.

- For five years, 1995–1999, Gordon won consecutive races at least once each season. He won three straight in 1996 and his four straight in 1998 tied a modern-era record.

- Gordon's 13 wins in 1998 equaled Petty's modern-era record.

- Gordon has led the Winston Cup Series in victories in five of the past eight seasons. Last season, in fact, broke a string of five consecutive years atop the leader board.

PACE LAP: JEFF GORDON

BY DAVID BOURNE
Stock Car Racing, October, 2001

I know that if I'm in a room full of race fans, I can say just two words to kick things up a notch: Jeff Gordon.

No other name in NASCAR Winston Cup racing sparks such heated debate between those who recognize and admire Gordon's accomplishments as one of the best drivers ever, and those who wouldn't pull for the guy even if their mother told them to.

When we started thinking about putting Gordon on the cover of *Stock Car Racing*, he wasn't burning up the track. He was decent, but hadn't reached his all-too-regular championship stride.

That didn't matter, however. Because when it comes to Gordon, regardless of where he's running on the track, or where he stands in points, the other drivers out there racing want to put him away. And many fans want the same thing.

If this were pro wrestling, fans would hope Gordon gets socked with a folding chair and stripped of his championship belt. If he were at a dunking booth, he'd have the longest line of people wanting to buy a ticket.

On the other hand, get this. If this were a pick-up game of racing, Gordon would be your first selection. Admit it. If you were to draw numbers at the track for a friendly bet on who wins, you would hope to pick the 24 car. You know good odds when you see them.

So just what is it that makes Gordon the man some guys want to beat or beat up on? For this story, we went to people like Darrell Waltrip to help find out. In Waltrip's heyday, the boos often rained down on him during driver introductions. He won often, and his mouth ran as fast as his race cars.

Waltrip says the problem with Gordon is one of envy among fellow competitors and fans. He sees a handsome, successful driver who has plenty of fame and fortune, not to mention a beautiful wife. Kind of the dream come true for many people.

"He looks like he could be a star in a movie," Waltrip says. "There's so many things about him that people are so envious of, and envy is the problem in our sport. The other competitors are envious. They want to be like Jeff Gordon, just like I was envious of Richard Petty. I wanted to be the King. I wanted to be the guy that they turned to, and I wanted to be the guy that everybody looked to.

"Being envious of a guy's position, most of us don't have the intelligence to attack somebody on an intellectual level. We go at them in a way to make them look bad."

A pretty honest assessment. And I totally agree. No, you won't find any No. 24 die-cast in my office. My motto isn't "refuse to lose." And I haven't been paired with Gordon for the next Winston No Bull $1 million bonus.

I just know that this guy can drive the wheels off a race car. And he's a heck of a nice guy off the track. Sure, I get as burned out as the next guy when the same driver wins all of the time. But the entire sport benefits when someone constantly challenges others to rise to the next level. And week-in and week-out, that person usually is Jeff Gordon.

So there you have it. Nothing less than a bull's-eye would work here. They might as well paint one on the bumper of Gordon's DuPont Chevrolet.

If you don't like Gordon, then the target practice is on us. If you do, don't be offended. Walk proudly into the racetrack, take your seat, and look around at the other fans. Rest assured that when it comes time to leave, you're the one most likely to go home with a grin on your face. That's because most of the other drivers will

ROBBIE LOOMIS

BY LARRY COTHREN
Stock Car Racing, January 2002

Robbie Loomis spent 11 years working for Petty Enterprises, nine years as crew chief, and helped put Bobby Hamilton and John Andretti in victory lane. During the 2001 season, in just his second year at Hendrick Motorsports, Loomis had Jeff Gordon back at the top of Winston Cup. In this interview with *Stock Car Racing*, Loomis talks about the effort needed to stay at the top of your game.

Tell us a little about your background, where you grew up, that sort of thing.

I grew up in Forest City, Florida. Actually, when I was 12 or 13, I would always go to my uncle's shop and work on his cars. Back then we didn't even have a trailer, so we would pull them to the race-track by chain. Then I started driving a little when I was 15 or 16, realized I couldn't afford that and started working on them and have been working on them ever since.

So racing has basically been a lifelong pursuit for you?

Oh yes, definitely. My father took me when I was so little, they tell me, that I can't even remember. They said I just liked the noise.

Your dad raced also?

He did it as a hobby years ago. Then I think he took the same route I did when I was 15 or 16 and decided he couldn't afford it and just started working on them and doing it more for enjoyment.

Where did you go after stepping away from your family's involvement in the sport?

A week after I graduated high school, I went to work for Mickey Gibbs and moved to Gadsden, Alabama. We ran the All Pro circuit and worked under a man named Ray Stonkus. That's really where I learned a lot about chassis setup, by working with Ray. Just one thing led to another after that.

Robby Loomis has crewed two of the greatest of the sport: Richard Petty and Jeff Gordon. *Sam Sharpe*

Loomis says he and driver Jeff Gordon have established the communication needed to win races. *Sam Sharpe*

When did you go to Petty Enterprises, and how exactly did that come about?

Actually, in 1987 we were doing some racing and bought engines from Prototype Engineering. Ron Neal was starting a Busch team with Kyle Petty, and called and wanted to know if I would be interested in taking care of it. He had Peak antifreeze and ran, I think, about 12 races that year. At the same time, Alan Kulwicki was going to run like seven races with Zerex antifreeze. It was kind of a unique thing that was out of the same shop up there in Hanesville, Illinois. So I talked to Ray Stonkus, who was my mentor at the time, about doing the thing and living up there. He said it would be a great opportunity because it would expose me to Kyle and the Pettys. I took it, and at the end of that season is when Kyle introduced me to his dad. One thing led to another from there.

If you had not achieved the success you have in this sport, would you still be involved in it? Would the motivation still be there?

The way I look at racing, I say all the time, is that racing has always been in my blood. It's been fun. I enjoy it as a hobby. I used to go Friday and Saturday nights all the time and wouldn't even get paid. I just like hearing the roar of the engines. I feel very fortunate that now I get paid for something I enjoy so much.

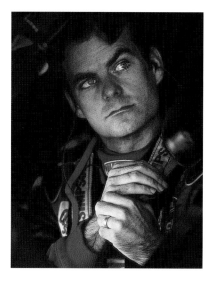

What are your hobbies outside of racing?

I love the sun and the beach, and I love to play golf. I only play about five or six games a year, but I love to play. That's probably about it.

Gordon handpicked Loomis to replace Ray Evernham as crew chief. *Nigel Kinrade*

If you weren't working in motorsports, what would you be doing right now?

I would probably be in the swimming pool business. My dad has a swimming pool business. I tell him all the time when we're having bad weeks, I'll check and say, "How's the swimming pool business doing?"

Do you try to emulate any one person in motorsports, especially someone in the mechanical/technological end of it?

There are always people who influence your life. I think going to the Pettys at such a young age and being under the influence of Richard and Dale Inman, they mold or shape your life in a certain way, shape your personality in a certain way. There are things to be learned from everyone. I try to realize that there's good in all things and all people. You have to look at the heart of everyone in every different situation.

Loomis says Hendrick Motorsports surrounds him with dedicated people.
Sam Sharpe

How does it feel to be on top of the sport right now?

I just feel very fortunate. Brooke and Jeff and I were talking recently about how there are a lot of people who work all their life, work every bit as hard as we do or our guys do, and they're never blessed with the results that we've been able to get. We're just very thankful and very fortunate to be in that situation.

How tough was last year when you replaced Ray Evernham and the team took somewhat of a downturn?

It was tough just because the expectations were as high as they were for this team last year. Coming into it, it was a hard adjustment for Jeff and a hard adjustment for me. I had been at a place 11 years and Jeff had been used to one guy telling him this and that for so long. Coming into a new environment, I think the one thing it showed me was how there are so many good people all around this earth and you never cross their paths. When I took this opportunity to come down here at Hendrick Motorsports and saw all the people on the team, it really made an impact on my life. You say, "Hey, there's a lot of great people out here who can work on cars."

What does it mean to you when Jeff Gordon says he handpicked you to be his crew chief?

It gives me a great feeling inside. I've said all along that the best thing about Jeff Gordon is not only his driving ability, but he is really a special person as far as his personality and how he cares about people. That really meant more to me, knowing what type of person he is, that he saw something he liked.

Which situation have you found to be more demanding, working at Petty Enterprises or at Hendrick Motorsports?

They're probably equally demanding. It's just different areas are demanding. At Petty Enterprises, we were just starting to be a multi-car team so there were a lot of different facets and things I was worried about. Here at Hendrick Motorsports, getting to work with Brian Whitesell and having a lot of things in place already, it takes a lot of pressure off of you in certain areas, but then there are added pressures from other areas because of the team's expectations and the job that's been done in the past. It's kind of funny because there are pressures I felt at Petty's I don't feel here, but then there are a lot of pressures here I feel that I didn't feel at Petty's. So there's kind of a balance in the pressure department.

The Pettys openly admit that they've fallen behind the times. Compared to Hendrick Motorsports, just how far behind would you say they've been?

I've said all along that this sport is a lot like a big clock. The hands are always moving. There are teams that are at the top, and you'll watch them and they'll cycle to the bottom. Then, if you watch them long enough, they'll cycle back to the top. As far as a single-car team, when we were at Petty Enterprises, we were really growing and gaining momentum. Then we came into the idea that to take it further we needed to step back a little bit, to take a little setback, to make it a multi-car team. As we did that, with a two-car team, it was going along pretty good.

Probably the biggest setback that's come along, and there's nothing anyone could do about it, was the loss of Adam. Adam was really going to be the one to carry the momentum, and the torch, from the driver's standpoint too. It takes a lot to find that right driver, to find that right mix. I know that Adam was a guy who had gobs and gobs of talent like these other guys, all these young guys, coming in—in addition to his experience of just being around the Thanksgiving table all those years of racing.

Take all of the Hendrick Motorsports drivers out of the mix and list the top three drivers out there today, strictly in terms of what they can get out of a race car.

Tony Stewart, Kevin Harvick, and probably Bobby Labonte. When you talk about talent in race car drivers, these guys keep getting these young guys coming in. I think Jeff is really the one who showed people, years ago when Mr. Hendrick got Jeff, that you can get these young guys. There are a lot of good racers out there running short tracks who keep raising the bar of competition because they understand the car and the equipment.

What one thing would you change about Winston Cup racing if you had the power to do so?

It's tough. I say all the time that I'll let NASCAR worry about that. It sees all the sides of it. We get caught up in just the competition part of it a lot of times. If I were in that position, though, I would try to work with the schedule so at least these Saturday-night events are spread out, where every third or fourth week you can at least give the road guys a break by having that Sunday off, and then try to schedule it where we don't have 20 races straight.

Where do you see the sport going in the next decade?

We had a lot of growth in the 1990s. The last couple of years the sport has leveled off a little bit, maybe. I think with this new TV package and a lot of things they're doing that are computerized on TV, probably within the next year, the next five years, it will be taken to the level where the fans are a lot more involved as they watch it on TV. I see it taking another rise up in the next five to seven years.

How much interaction do you have with the other Hendrick crew chiefs, Tony Furr and Gary DeHart?

We interact all the time. Tony Furr and Gary DeHart both, they've been a tremendous help to us all year. It comes back to that saying that I try to listen to everybody. It's good to listen to Terry (Labonte) and Jerry (Nadeau) too, because they feel things different in a race car than Jeff will. A lot of times they'll be trying different things in practice than we are. A lot of times—on several occasions this year—we'll start the race with something we've got from Terry's or Jerry's situation in their car, and it will help us.

Is that a key to the success at Hendrick Motorsports, the communication you have in-house?

Hendrick Motorsports surrounds you with so many tools. With Jeff Gordon, the nice part about it is [that] when we go to every racetrack we know we have the best driver in the world in our car. I have the mentality that with Jeff we should be capable of being in contention to win every race. Mr. Hendrick supplies us with the tools and surrounds us with the people around us so Brian and I can go out there and get the job done with Jeff.

Where do you see yourself 5 years, 10 years, down the road?

You know, I consider myself a pretty loyal and stable person. I said before I came over here that if I made the move I wanted to make sure it was going to be for a while and not just a little while. Somewhere involved heavily with racing. I'm sure 10 years from now I won't want to be down there under the microscope and the pressure cooker calling all the shots on the crew chief part of it, but who knows from there?

NO BOUNDARIES

BY BRUCE MARTIN
Stock Car Racing, March 2002

Few Obstacles in the Way of Jeff Gordon Reaching a Championship Milestone

It wasn't long after Jeff Gordon won his fourth NASCAR Winston Cup title that the question was asked: Now that Gordon has won four titles by the age of 30, can he win four more to become the first eight-time Winston Cup champion?

Unless something dramatic happens to Gordon, it appears certain that the Hendrick Motorsports driver will achieve that goal by the end of his career.

What makes four more titles so important is it would surpass Richard Petty and the late Dale Earnhardt, the two drivers who share the NASCAR record of seven Winston Cup championships.

"My goal in life's not to get seven or eight championships," Gordon says. "My goals constantly change, and I want to continue to be competitive and successful in this business and that is not always going to mean that you are winning the championship. I want to give this team everything that I can, and I want to see them getting everything out of themselves that they can and be proud of what they have accomplished and having fun.

"As hectic as life is and this business is, we have to try to enjoy it and have fun. To me, that overrides whether or not we accomplish eight championships or seven championships."

As Gordon continues to become the dominant driver of his era, part of his charm is his "aw shucks" humility. It would be easy for Gordon to point to his tremendous accomplishments as a driver, but he is just as amazed as anybody else at what he has accomplished in a Winston Cup career that began with the final race of the 1992 season.

That is why he genuinely believes winning four more titles is a tremendous obstacle, while others believe it's only a matter of time.

"I have no idea if I can get four more because I wasn't expecting to get the fourth," Gordon says. "Last season was somewhat of a surprise. It was a great year. I think we knew we were going to have

Nigel Kinrade

a much better year than we had in 2000, but I don't think we had any idea we were going to be coming out and doing what we have done.

"Anything is possible, but it has taken an awful lot to get four. I know it has happened quick in your minds, but to me it's been a lot of hard work and dedication to get that. If we stay committed and we continue to have the resources, I hope I have that same drive to do it."

Early Greatness

To those who have to compete against Gordon nearly every week, they understand why he is the best driver in NASCAR. And at least one living legend believes Gordon will win four more titles and become the sport's first eight-time Winston Cup champion.

"It's just how long he wants to do it," Richard Petty says. "If he wants to go for eight championships, then he can probably get them. But he started so early you wonder when he will get burned out on all of this. He's the only one that is even close to being able to do it right now with his youth and the team he has around him. It's very, very possible he can win four more as far as that is concerned."

Benny Parsons won the 1973 NASCAR Winston Cup championship when the season title was based on miles completed. Since that time, the point structure has been changed to reward consistency.

Parsons raced against Petty when he was the dominant driver in the 1970s, and competed against Earnhardt in the 1980s. He also saw Earnhardt's greatness continue in the 1990s when Parsons was a television analyst for ESPN and ABC Sports.

Now, as a member of NBC Sports, Parsons can appreciate the greatness that Gordon has displayed at such an early age.

"There is no doubt that he can rewrite most of the records except the 200 wins," Parsons says, referring to Petty's 200 career victories. "Obviously, I don't think he is going to achieve that, but most of the other records, he should be able to.

"The reason for Jeff Gordon's success is he has a tremendous feel for the car. He is able to come in and tell the crew chief what the car is doing so they can fix it. He is a huge part of the success of that team. Everyone gave Ray Evernham the credit for Jeff Gordon's first three titles when he was Jeff's crew chief. Evernham deserved a lot of credit, but they have won races since he left and they have won a championship since he left.

"Jeff Gordon is a tremendous talent, plus he understands what to do. When Ray Evernham left, Jeff Gordon stepped up to become a bigger part of that. He is not an idiot. He knew he had to step up and he did."

Near-Perfect Seasons

Since Gordon won his first Winston Cup title in 1995, the only drivers who have won the championship since are Terry Labonte in 1996, Dale Jarrett in 1999, and Bobby Labonte in 2000.

Jarrett knows it takes almost a perfect season to win the championship, and Gordon has often driven near perfection throughout his career. That is why Jarrett believes four more titles are Gordon's, if he really wants them.

"It depends on how long he wants to go at this," Jarrett says. "If you look at where Dale Earnhardt was, almost 50 years old and still very competitive, Jeff definitely has 15 more years he could do this, and with his talent he could win a lot more in this sport.

"You can do it, you just have to have almost a perfect year like what I did and what Bobby Labonte did in 2000. You have to put it all together for a long period of time. They have proven they can do that. You can do it, but it is becoming more and more difficult. For as good a year as they have had, they were struggling at the end of the season."

Jarrett came up in an era when drivers breaking into Winston Cup racing had to start with a bottom-rung team before getting a chance to move up to a better operation. Jarrett struggled with lesser teams before he finally earned a chance to compete for the Wood Brothers, where he scored his first victory in 1991.

That earned him an opportunity to race for team owner Joe Gibbs, and he would go on to win the 1993 Daytona 500. Two years later, Jarrett joined Robert Yates Racing and would ultimately score his only Winston Cup championship in 1999.

By contrast, Gordon began his Winston Cup career at Hendrick Motorsports working with Evernham, one of the brightest crew chiefs of his era.

"It makes a difference whenever you can get in good equipment from the beginning. Your learning curve is much shorter," Jarrett says. "You learn how to win and drive top-notch equipment from the very beginning rather than struggling through that time. Your confidence goes up and it is easier to find your way to the top and get yourself with a winning organization like that from the beginning."

When Evernham left Hendrick Motorsports in September 1999 to begin a project that would lead Dodge back into the sport after a two-decade absence, Gordon continued to win races, but the team faltered from its championship status.

> *Mention NASCAR today, and the immediate vision is Gordon driving the No. 24 Chevrolet to another checkered flag.*

Gordon helped persuade Robbie Loomis to join Hendrick Motorsports as the crew chief beginning in 2000 and the combination reached fruition in 2001.

"They are both very talented, but you have to figure they are going to work well together," Jarrett says. "They both have a lot of talent, a lot of respect for each other. When you put talent together, you are going to have good results."

While Jarrett admits Gordon has the look of greatness, team owner Robert Yates isn't about to claim Gordon as an eight-time champion in waiting.

"If we take the attitude that he is going to whip us all the time, he probably will," Yates says. "We are going to go get him next year. He can't win next year.

"He is good, he is great. He has awesome equipment and he's an awesome driver. But he can be beat. That is what our plans are. We are going to beat the little sucker."

The competitive side of Yates wants to beat Gordon, but he also has a deep appreciation for what makes the driver great.

"Jeff Gordon brings everything he needs to as a driver," Yates says. "Rick Hendrick provides everything he needs to in the equipment with some great people there and a great organization. They are just flat tough to beat anyway."

Petty was the face of NASCAR racing during his lengthy racing career. The mere mention of NASCAR conjured up visions of Petty driving the famous No. 43 at Daytona and other circuits on the schedule.

Mention NASCAR today, and the immediate vision is Gordon driving the No. 24 Chevrolet to another checkered flag.

"I think he is really good for the sport," Petty says. "When it first started, you had some people, but you didn't have any press. I came along and didn't have that much press, but I filled up a gap. Then, you had Dale Earnhardt come along and he fills up a gap. Now, you have Jeff Gordon taking it from one era into another era.

"Right now, he is our spokesperson, as far as racing is concerned, because that's our winner. He is doing a good job. We have so many new fans who don't know how rough it used to be. They look at football, baseball, and basketball. I think he brings it up to a new level of awareness with the new fans."

Tackling Stock Cars

To be compared to Richard Petty and Dale Earnhardt is quite an honor to a young driver who was headed to an Indy car career in the late 1980s. Gordon moved from California to Pittsboro, Indiana, as a teenager for a chance to continue his open-wheel racing career in the 1980s.

"I always knew the name Richard Petty, but I just didn't follow stock car racing that much," Gordon says. "If I just go back ten years ago, or even fifteen years ago, stock car racing was still something that was looked at as a southeastern kind of thing. A lot of us didn't know how huge it was or the fan base that it had.

"Growing up in California, I didn't know much about it. To me, it was all about sprint cars because that is what was going on around my area and it was all about the Indianapolis 500."

Then one day Gordon had a conversation with a man who put an idea into his head.

"What really got it started for me was Larry Nuber," Gordon says of the late television broadcaster. "Because he did some commentating on ESPN on NASCAR races, he asked me if I had thought about stock cars. I said I hadn't. He told me I really needed to try to drive one. I asked how I would do that and he told me about the Buck Baker Driving School.

Gordon's on track talent is matched by his charisma. He led the sport to a new era. *Sam Sharpe*

"So I went down there and said, 'Man, I love this. This is cool. This is an awesome racetrack at Rockingham. It's got high banks; it's fast. Man, this is what I like, right here.'

"That's when I locked onto NASCAR. I started watching and listening to everything that I could. Unfortunately, it was toward the end of Richard's career. That is why I got criticized in 1993 and 1994, maybe even 1995, not knowing the history of the sport and all that Richard Petty had done. I've had to educate myself since then."

Gordon's first Winston Cup race came in the final race of Petty's career. It was the last race of the 1992 season, and Gordon drove the No. 24 DuPont Chevrolet in a 500-mile race at Atlanta Motor Speedway in preparation for his 1993 rookie season. It's as if the baton was being handed from the outgoing king to the boy king.

"People were saying, this is Jeff Gordon's first race and he may be somebody to watch in the future and here is Richard Petty's last race," Gordon says. "Maybe it was just because I was the new guy that day. I don't know, but it was very cool to be mentioned in the same sentence that day, and it was pretty cool for me to be a part of that event because it was Richard's last event. I got a chance to see him in action, in the garage area, on the racetrack, and to experience that is something that I'll never forget."

1995

Gordon wins his first NASCAR Winston Cup championship. In doing so, he becomes the youngest champion in the modern era. Highlights include 7 wins, 8 poles, 17 top 5s, and 23 top 10s.

1997

Gordon wins his second championship. He becomes the first driver to earn more than $6 million in a season and the youngest driver to win the Daytona 500. Other highlights include 10 wins (for second consecutive season), 1 pole, 22 top 5s, and 23 top 10s.

1998

Gordon wins his third championship in four years, and second straight. He ties Richard Petty for the modern era season-win record, with 13 victories, and ties the modern era record with four consecutive victories. He sets a record with earnings of $9.3 million. Other highlights include 7 poles, 26 top 5s, and 28 top 10s.

2001

Gordon wins his fourth championship, becoming the youngest driver in Winston Cup history to do so. Only Dale Earnhardt and Richard Petty hold more championships. Highlights include 6 wins, 8 poles, 18 top 5s, and 24 top 10s.

Dueling With Dale

Gordon only had one opportunity to race against Petty, but he enjoyed many battles with Earnhardt.

"Dale Earnhardt was in his prime when I started thinking about driving," Gordon says. "To me, Dale Earnhardt was a bigger name at the time than Richard Petty was because he was the guy winning championships at that time. To come and race against him was something.

"I don't think I ever appreciated him by just hearing about him or watching him on TV. It was when I got to race against him and see just how good I was."

Gordon says the one thing he missed most about winning his fourth Winston Cup title was having Earnhardt come up to him and give him one of his famous pinches or headlocks.

"You get caught up in what goes on here every weekend and you don't necessarily get a chance to think and reflect on that," he says. "The times I had with Dale and the great races we had, I miss that.

"Nobody is ever going to be able to replace that."

Washed up at 29

When Gordon clinched his fourth Winston Cup title in a career that began just nine years ago, the 30-year-old driver could have been excused if he had a message for all of his detractors.

TOPS AT 30

A comparison of what Richard Petty, Dale Earnhardt, and Jeff Gordon accomplished as of their 30th birthday

Driver	Starts	Championships	Poles	Wins	Top 5s	Top 10s
Richard Petty	358	1	57	60	189	238
Dale Earnhardt	76	1	4	6	34	48
Jeff Gordon	277	3	38	55	141	179

* Gordon turned 30 just prior to the 2001 Brickyard 400 at Indy.
** Petty won his fourth Winston Cup championship at the age of 35. Earnhardt won his fourth championship at the age of 39.

In 2000, when Gordon was struggling to a ninth-place finish in the series and was no longer the driver to beat in nearly every race, the anti-Gordon crowd crowed that without Evernham as his crew chief, Gordon's glory days were over.

Nothing could have been more absurd. It was just a matter of time before Gordon regained his championship luster.

Gordon says, "You have to love the critics. They are writing what is on their minds and they can inspire you in a lot of ways. They certainly inspired me and this team."

Gordon's Winston Cup titles in 1995, 1997, and 1998 came with Evernham in charge of the team at Hendrick Motorsports. Together, they formed one of the best crew chief/driver combinations in NASCAR history.

Gordon's fourth title was with Loomis as the crew chief.

"This championship is a lot different than the first three," Gordon says. "The year is so special because of the last two years. We had to rebuild and we had to come together, basically, as a new team. We had to climb the mountain again.

"Because of all the adversity we have had to overcome the last couple of years, it has made this year even sweeter."

By scoring his fourth Winston Cup title by the age of 30, Gordon is halfway home to breaking the record of seven titles shared by Petty and Earnhardt.

Are four more titles a realistic goal? Gordon has been too busy enjoying his latest title to give it much thought.

"This is blowing me away," he says. "It hasn't sunk in yet. We want to get it done first, then I can start reflecting on the year and what has gone on in my career. I'm just pretty proud to have four.

"It's been an amazing ride."

STILL THE MAN TO BEAT

BY THOMAS POPE
Stock Car Racing, April 2003

Jeff Gordon Puts a Rough Year Behind Him and Focuses on What He Does Best

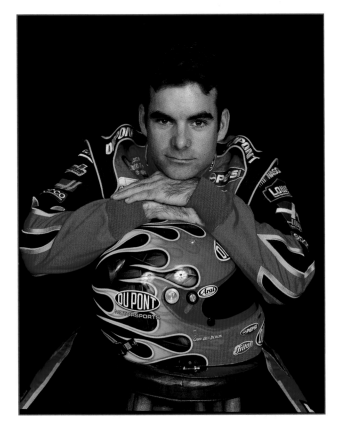

Harold Hinson

Jeff Gordon's career path indelibly stamps him as an extreme thrill seeker. But the 2002 NASCAR Winston Cup season, one in which he had high hopes of repeating as champion, turned out to be a roller coaster ride that would have left even the hardiest soul weak-kneed.

Up-and-down performance on the track, coupled with his wife Brooke filing for divorce, tested Gordon's mettle in ways he never imagined. At the low point of the campaign, crew chief Robbie Loomis had serious concerns about keeping his job at Hendrick Motorsports.

Despite the turmoil, Gordon had a legitimate chance to successfully defend his crown, and all three of his victories came in the final third of the season. That late surge and the potential of a redesigned Monte Carlo SS boosted the confidence of Gordon's team. The 31-year-old driver believes a fifth Winston Cup championship is there for the taking in 2003.

"I want to get my personal stuff behind me. That's not going to happen anytime soon, unfortunately; but now it's not affecting me as much as it was during part of 2002," Gordon says. "I'm kind of just living my life and getting focused to go out and do it [in 2003]. Sometimes success is not as far out of your grasp as you think."

Dodging Distractions

Gordon can say that in hindsight, having rebounded from as low as 11th in the 2002 points to finish 4th. He went 31 races between wins—from September 30, 2001, until August 24, 2002—an agonizing drought that nearly left the team in tatters. Making matters worse were the constant questions about whether the distractions of divorce proceedings and co-ownership of the team headed by rookie driver Jimmie Johnson had left Gordon unable to focus on his own racing. The edge Gordon had in winning four championships from 1995–2001 seemed to have been lost.

Yet, according to Loomis, it was Gordon who played the primary role in getting the team back on track.

"Jeff was the one all year who calmed the waters," Loomis says. "When we weren't winning, everybody was freaking out. He said, 'Hey, we sat down in December after the banquet and we didn't talk about winning races; we talked about winning a second straight championship and helping Jimmie win rookie of the year.'

He kept us looking at the goal of what we were working toward, and that kind of calmed us for a little bit."

The 2002 season started off decently enough for Gordon, with lead-lap finishes in the first four events and a pair of Top 10s.

But then, in March, Brooke Gordon, Jeff's wife of seven years, filed for divorce, citing "marital misconduct"—a Florida legal term that covers a multitude of alleged transgressions. The fact that Jeff and Brooke appeared to be the picture-perfect couple—young, dashing championship driver and ravishing former Miss Winston—only made the news of the breakup more intriguing.

Gordon refuses to discuss the particulars of what led to the separation, but he's open about how his marriage upheaval affected him.

"I don't think it was as hard as dealing with the pressure of not winning," Gordon says. "When it keeps being brought up that you haven't won in twenty-five races, thirty races, that stuff starts to affect you. Each week that goes by without winning, it gets tougher and tougher and tougher.

"When a certain number of races went by, then they [the fans and media] started wondering, is it the personal issues? I can't really say that the personal side of things was preventing us from winning races. We were in position and had things break or had wrecks happen. I don't see how anyone could possibly say my personal life caused that. But the stuff going on in my personal life compounded what was happening on the track and made for a tougher first half of the year."

Early into their marriage, Jeff and Brooke Gordon appeared to be the perfect couple—a racing superstar in the making and a gorgeous, former Miss Winston. When Brooke filed for divorce in 2002, the press questioned Jeff about whether his personal life was to blame for a slip in his performance at the track.
SCR Archives/Harold Hinson

While the entanglements of divorce were a daily consideration, if not a distraction, for Gordon, when he got in the car, racing was his sole focus, Loomis says.

"I tell people all the time, whatever was in the car, he got all of it out of it," Loomis says. "When he got out of the car, he had to think about what was going on with the divorce stuff. But when he was in the car, he was one hundred percent into it."

Racing provided Gordon with what he called "an amazing kind of therapy," and so did his parents, team owner Rick Hendrick, and others whose opinion he could trust.

"I never allowed the distractions to really affect me in my work with driving the race car," Gordon says. "I don't think people can really understand that unless you get behind the wheel of a car and drive as hard as we do.

"I always put my faith in God and allowed him to guide me. I'm not somebody who dwells on problems and worries too much, but certainly I'm going to talk to people about certain issues—people I respect and trust."

Down to Business

At the same time, however, Loomis had to re-examine his relationship with Gordon in order to cure an on-track disease called "mediocrity." Through the end of May, Gordon had managed only three Top-5 finishes.

When Gordon and company stumbled in 2002, the fall was huge, including uncharacteristic problems under the hood. *Harold Hinson*

"For the first two years, we had strictly a business relationship, but then that evolved into a friendship as well," Loomis says. "And I was trying to be careful about that because I'm friends with both Jeff and Brooke. And then you see what happens with Bobby Labonte and (crew chief) Jimmy Makar, who are two of the best in the business. They were really good friends, but eventually I think that hurt their racing. It was kind of the same thing with Jeff and me, and by about the third or fourth month, we got back around to mostly a business relationship because that's what we, as a team, needed."

By that point, Gordon and Loomis were painfully aware that they had lost ground in a sport that never stands still. Human nature set in, and the fear of fixing what wasn't broken came back to haunt the team on race day. They didn't fall behind the rest of the pack because they were liberal in their thinking, but because they weren't getting radical enough, Gordon says. "We were using setups that worked well for us in 2001—setups that won six races and a championship. That's proof of how fast things develop and how you've got to be ready to expand and grow and move."

Loomis says history should have taught him to be unafraid of being bold. In his short tenure at Hendrick Motorsports, he had already experienced the pitfalls of conservatism in Gordon's chassis options.

When Loomis left Petty Enterprises after the 1999 season and signed on as Gordon's crew chief, he was understandably leery about being too pushy too soon. The result was relatively catastrophic, as Gordon finished ninth in points—his worst showing in the standings since his 1993 rookie season.

During that off-season, Loomis and his short-term predecessor, Brian Whitesell, agreed to take a new approach to Gordon's setups for 2001. The change of battle plans resulted in twice as many victories (six) as Gordon scored in 2000, 18 top-5 finishes, a championship, and nearly $11 million in earnings.

A Rookie Guide

In spite of the one-year turnaround, Gordon's team fell victim to human nature and got conservative again. Magnifying Gordon's on-track problems was the immediate success of Johnson and his crew chief, Chad Knaus.

As a first-year pairing, they weren't shackled by tradition and didn't feel compelled to follow established Hendrick

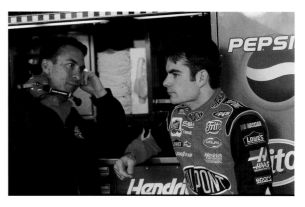

Crew chief Robbie Loomis (left) blames many of the team's struggles on a hesitation to step outside of the comfort zone and try new setups. *Sam Sharpe*

Gordon became a car owner in 2001, and often was upstaged by his protege Jimmie Johnson. *Sam Sharpe*

blueprints. Their ideas worked in ways that Gordon's and Loomis' didn't, and Johnson consistently outperformed his teammate/boss. Johnson scored his first Winston Cup victory on April 28 at California Speedway, and then won again on June 2 at Dover.

With the latter win, Johnson took over second in the point standings with Gordon one spot back. But Gordon still didn't seem to be hitting on all cylinders, and he and Loomis agreed to rely less on the past and more on the present, in effect casting their lot with Johnson and Knaus.

"They were going against the grain with setups, and they had so much success the first of the year," Loomis says. "We weren't winning, and we needed to open our minds to those kinds of different things that Jimmie and Chad were doing."

Loomis admits that changing course was a way of saving his own skin.

"We're in the performance business, and I know that, like a head coach in the NFL or the NBA, we get paid to perform," Loomis says. "There was a time when I was very concerned over my future. I knew I'd have a job somewhere in Winston Cup racing, but I wasn't sure whether it would be with Hendrick Motorsports or Jeff Gordon. I felt like we had a good team, but having two cars in-house made things different across the board."

The breakthrough came as the circuit returned to its southern roots for a late-summer run. Gordon ended his drought at Bristol, leading the most laps and then shoving Rusty Wallace out of the lead to capture the Sharpie 500. The win, also an end to the losing streak, was a huge relief to Gordon and Loomis. "Bristol brought me off the respirator," Loomis says. "I was breathing on my own again after that."

A week later, Gordon was back in victory lane, this time in the Southern 500 at Darlington, where he led all but three of the final 127 laps. It was Gordon's fifth victory in NASCAR's oldest superspeedway

Gordon has shown he can tame even the toughest racetracks. He visited victory lane three times in 2003 as he returned to championship form. *SCR Archives*

event, tying the mark held by Cale Yarborough. It also moved Gordon into second in the points, just 91 markers behind the leader, Sterling Marlin.

But just as quickly as the team found its groove, it lost it—big-time. Gordon's engine broke the following Saturday night at Richmond, and then he could only muster a 14th-place finish at New Hampshire. The next week, at Dover, Gordon ran poorly and then was swept up in a crash.

A win a week later at Kansas City was followed by yet another blown engine at Talladega, and that 42nd-place finish was the death knell to his title hopes. He finished 36th at Martinsville after being shoved into the backstretch, then rebounded to finish 6th, 5th, 3rd, and 5th to end the season and capture 4th in the points. The finale at Homestead saw him start from 37th—the first time in his career that he had used a provisional to make the field.

"Every season's different," Gordon says. "You never know what it's going to take or who's going to get on a roll. When we won Bristol and Darlington back to back, I think everybody thought, 'Shoot, here we go on a run to the championship.' Then we had a couple of the worst weeks we had all year long.

"You never take anything for granted. You go all out, hope it's your year, and do the things you think that it takes to get on top. You've got to fight from the first race to the last race. There's not one point in the season that you race for points or do things where you let up.

"That's probably what's changed most about our sport in recent years. I mean, you not only have to fight hard every race, you fight hard every lap of every race. Six or seven years ago, you could save tires, save the car, cars would fall out and all you had to do was be there at end; if you played smart, you'd be there at the end of race. Now you've got pit strategy involved in ways that it wasn't before, you've got cars that are stuck like glue the whole tire run because of the downforce the cars make, and the tires last forever. A lot has changed, and it's tough to keep up with all of it all of the time."

A Season of Change

More changes were in store for 2003. Some in Gordon's pit crew have been replaced, and then there's the learning curve inherent in a redesigned Chevrolet Monte Carlo SS. Those kinds of regular shakeups, Loomis says, help to keep a team excited about its short- and long-term tasks.

"The new car has better balance, downforce-wise, front to rear and with less drag, and that's what we've been up against with Dodge and Ford the past two years," Loomis says. "We're pretty excited to be able to come out with a package like that and compete on more equal terms."

Loomis believes the Chevy camp should whip the Monte Carlo into shape quickly thanks in part to the defection of Joe Gibbs Racing (the title team in 2000 and 2002) to the Chevy contingent.

"The new Chevrolet and the new (Pontiac) Grand Prix should help the GM teams a lot when it comes to racing in traffic," Loomis says. "For the last two years, if we were out front, we were extra strong, but if you got behind somebody, you couldn't get around them. I think the 2003 Monte Carlo and Grand Prix will definitely bring some parity between the manufacturers."

And as if those changes weren't enough to keep a team stoked, there's always Gordon's rock-solid confidence that he can do special things with a race car.

"You go through times when you work just as hard at doing everything the same and it's just not happening," Gordon says. "You just start to question a lot of things. My confidence in my driving, I don't think that I ever really questioned that."

Neither did Loomis, who gives his driver all the credit for keeping the team from coming apart at the seams during the low points of 2002.

"We all know what a winner is and he's the one all along who kept us calm," Loomis says. "A lot of drivers have asked me what the difference is between Jeff Gordon and other drivers. I think that having won four championships, Jeff has confidence that runs way deep."

As Gordon continues to mature (remember, he's only 31, with four championships under his belt in only 10 seasons), he will continue to exhibit even more leadership, especially as a team co-owner.

"I'm at the shop more now because I'm a bigger part of the organization than I used to be," Gordon says. "I have more of a say in things now and a hand in what's going on, but to be honest with you, my role really hasn't changed all that much. I'm the driver of the number twenty-four DuPont Chevrolet, and other than having four Winston Cup championships and sixty-one wins, nothing's changed.

Gordon struggled to stay out front in 2002, but a new body style for the Monte Carlo provided a big boost in 2003.
Sam Sharpe

OPENING THE BOOKS

Jeff Gordon's divorce proceedings forced him to give the public a personal look into his finances. In court papers, Gordon says he earns $1.87 million per month, and estimates his worth at $48.8 million.

Gordon says in the court documents that his gross monthly income includes $29,683 in base salary, $800,000 in bonuses, $579,564 in income from corporations and partnerships, $11,582 in interest, $434,540 in income from royalties or trusts, $10,263 in personal expenses reimbursed by his corporations or given in lieu of income, and $991 from retirement plans.

Gordon says he is building a $1 million condominium, and pays $4,500 a month to rent a condominium in Charlotte. He lists monthly charitable donations of $8,900.

"That's all the role I want right now. I love being involved from the ownership side of things and I try to be as much of a teammate as I can to the other drivers here, but they know my involvement in getting Jimmie's team going. When I want to step away from driving, that's when my role around here will change significantly."

Gordon is many years from hanging up his helmet. He knows that his role as one of the sport's giants has opened many doors for him, including guest host stints on *Live with Regis and Kelly* and *Saturday Night Live*.

Even at his young age, Gordon is already seventh on the list of all-time Winston Cup race winners, and he is only 23 victories away from tying Bobby Allison and Darrell Waltrip for third place. David Pearson's second-best mark of 105 wins is a possibility, though probably a tougher mountain to climb than tying, or surpassing, the record of seven Winston Cup crowns shared by Richard Petty and Dale Earnhardt.

"The competition is stiffer now than ever before," team founder and owner Rick Hendrick says. "But if we can control the failures and finish every race, we can leave the rest of it up to Jeff Gordon."

THE HENDRICK MOTORSPORTS TRAGEDY

BY RON LEMASTERS JR.
Stock Car Racing, February 2005

On a day that held so much promise, so much optimism for the future of Hendrick Motorsports and its NASCAR racing teams, the news that a company plane had crashed into the side of a Virginia mountain came with devastating force.

The plane, carrying 10 passengers and crew, was on its way to Martinsville Speedway for the Subway 500 on October 24, traveling through thick fog near the Blue Ridge Airport when it crashed. Among those killed were Ricky Hendrick, son of team owner Rick; John Hendrick, president of the Hendrick organization, and his twin daughters, Jennifer and Kimberly; Jeff Turner, the company's general manager; Randy Dorton, head of the company's engine department; Joe Jackson, head of DuPont's racing program; Scott Lathram, who flew helicopters for Tony Stewart; and pilots Dick Tracy and Liz Morrison.

Randy Dorton's engines helped power Jeff Gordon to four Cup championships.
Nigel Kinrade

Ricky (center) was responsible for bringing Brian Vickers (right) to Hendrick Motorsports. Vickers promptly won the 2003 Busch Series title. Kyle Busch is on the left. *SCR Archives*

The shocking news reverberated throughout the racing community, somewhat like when Dale Earnhardt was killed at Daytona in 2001. Because Earnhardt was the biggest star in the biggest racing series in the country, his death was a hammer blow.

To Hendrick Motorsports, the effects are easily as far-reaching. Earnhardt was the man in control of Dale Earnhardt Inc., but his wife Teresa and son Dale Jr. stepped in immediately to assume control with the help of faithful lieutenants. In the case of the Hendrick tragedy, it was that cadre of lieutenants were among those lost.

Never before in NASCAR's rich history has such a tragedy occurred. There have been instances where one or two members of a team have been lost in air crashes, such as Alan Kulwicki and Davey Allison who were killed in separate incidents, but never before have so many key personnel involved in a single team been lost at once.

One has to go back to the tragic air crash that all but obliterated the senior leadership of the United States Auto Club in the late 1970s to find such an occurrence in the annals of motorsports. Outside motorsports, Marshall University lost its entire football team in an air crash in 1970, and Evansville University in Indiana lost its basketball team in a similar incident in 1977. The recovery, if such a thing is possible in an event of this magnitude, took many years for all three.

Perhaps the most direct comparison is Petty Enterprises, which lost its future when Adam Petty was killed in a crash during practice at New Hampshire in 2000. The team, owned by Adam's grandfather Richard, had just lost its patriarch, Richard's father Lee, and was being run by Adam's father Kyle. All the plans the team had for its future were in ruins, as was the Petty family, but in time the grief stabilized and the team got back to the business of racing as it had for the past 50-plus years.

Hendrick driver Jimmie Johnson had not even finished his burnout after winning at Martinsville before NASCAR and team officials were on the scene, ushering the drivers, teams, and other personnel away from the frenzied crowd to deliver the somber news.

In the weeks following the crash, grief was the primary emotion displayed by the NASCAR community. Later, when feelings weren't quite so raw, thoughts turned to how the Hendrick organization would cope with the loss of its key personnel, including two-thirds of its present leadership in John Hendrick and Turner, plus its future leader in 24-year-old Ricky Hendrick.

While no immediate moves were made, the sheer magnitude of the loss suffered by Hendrick Motorsport leaves one of the sport's premier organizations with several unanswered questions.

"I will say right now I think there are so many things going through all of our minds," said four-time series champion Jeff Gordon prior to the race at Atlanta in October, one week after the tragic plane crash. "We're still in such shock. It's been just something that has been, you know, just unbearable for anybody to deal with, and getting through something like this is going to take time. It is going to take a lot of support."

Support is one thing the Hendrick organization had in great numbers following the tragedy. Thousands of fans visited the Hendrick shops near Lowe's Motor Speedway to leave flowers, mementos, and messages of support to the stricken team. "I want to thank those people out there who have been so supportive and given their thoughts and their prayers for the families, for those who have been left behind through this, [because] those are the things that are going to get them through this, and yeah, there is a time when you have to move on," Gordon said. "I don't know when that time is. Losing, you know, whether it be a mother, father, sister, brother, in this way, I just . . . I don't know how we're going . . . anybody is going to move past that, but as far as we're concerned here, we do have a job at hand. We want to keep that legacy going."

Perhaps the most tragic victim of the crash was young Ricky Hendrick, who was being groomed to step into his father's role as the owner of Hendrick Motorsports. The 24-year-old was a bright, energetic young man with unlimited potential, given those he had to learn from and the legacy to which he was heir.

A former driver, Ricky was responsible for the grooming of young Brian Vickers, who was in his rookie season in Nextel Cup. Ricky was the spotter in Vickers' ear all day long at every race. The 21-year-old Vickers dealt with the loss of his friend, but it was not easy. He did not answer questions at the "remembrance" conference at Atlanta the week following the crash.

John Hendrick, who stepped into his brother's place when Rick was diagnosed with leukemia and carried on the Hendrick tradition to two NASCAR Nextel Cup championships, was remembered as a quiet leader who kept the team headed in the right direction during another trying time.

"I think a lot of people didn't know John very well until he came on the scene there," said Terry Labonte, driver of the No. 5 Kellogg's Chevrolet for Hendrick. "I don't think there was anybody that could have stepped in and done the job that John did besides John. Rick was sick and wasn't able to be a part of the team there for a while. John stepped in; I mean, the place never missed a beat with his leadership and

In less than five
months, Rick
Hendrick (far right)
lost (from left) his
son Ricky, his father
Joe, and his brother
John. *Harold Hinson*

his ability to take that team forward and just move on with it. I think he was truly the only guy who could have stepped in and done the job that he did. He immediately gained the confidence of everybody there, everybody respected him and looked up to him, and, you know, when he said something, they listened. So he was quite a guy to be able to come in and do that."

Gordon, who has been with Hendrick the longest (12 seasons), said the family would overcome the tragedy in time. "Every member of that family, the Hendrick family, has a special quality about them that you just don't find every day," Gordon said. "They all have it. And John, he did an amazing job coming in there, and he was more than just a face. He was active and had his heart into it as well, and his heart just continued to grow in motorsports. He loved being a part of it. And just like I said, they treated everyone with such respect, and they earned such respect because of the way they treated people, and our whole organization—his family, and everyone who's been in this whole event were family. That's the thing that's making it so tough, but it's also the thing that's going to help us continue to move on."

Jeff Turner was the man who dealt with all the day-to-day issues facing a business that employs nearly 500 people. He was the Hendrick family's man on the inside, and by all accounts he was very good at his job.

Randy Dorton was the man who put a name to Hendrick horsepower. It was his mechanical know-how and genius that enabled Hendrick to put more power on the racetrack than his rivals, and it was he who spread that power around the garage area. In addition to the four cars fielded by Hendrick, those driven by Ward Burton, Scott Riggs, and Joe Nemechek also made use of Dorton engines.

How will Hendrick overcome the loss of not only key personnel, but his only son and his brother? That is a question that will be answered only as time goes on. How it affected Gordon and Johnson's efforts toward winning the 2004 Nextel Cup is a matter of public record.

Johnson's victory at Martinsville on that fateful day was his second straight, and he rebounded for a victory at Atlanta the following weekend. Gordon, who has been in championship battles many of his 12 seasons, rededicated himself to the task of winning this one, the most important of his life.

"I have never been so inspired and driven in my life," he said at Atlanta. "This is an important weekend for us for so many reasons, but I can't think of anything that could drive us harder and stronger than this loss. One, we want it bad no matter what. We work very hard for it, but I think there is something that's going to allow us to dig a little deeper to try to make a difference, whether it be for the families that are grieving, to try to ease their pain some, or for those who are, you know, looking down on us. I think that instead of this being something that's a negative, we're going to take something and make something positive out of it and try to do our jobs better than we ever have before."

Robbie Loomis, Gordon's crew chief, has known loss before. He was part of Petty Enterprises that day at New Hampshire when Adam Petty died. "I think it would be a great story to win this championship. The biggest thing that's going to help is the support for one another, the love we can give to one another every day, and just doing our job," Loomis said. "That's what they'd want us to do, and we're going to do it well."

Such tragedy, when viewed through the prism of long experience, is a self-forging event. At such times, tragedy tends to draw friends and family in close so as to share the burden of crushing grief. Imagine having to go back to work 36 hours later in the midst of a championship fight, as the Hendrick group did.

The fallout from the tragic events of October 24, 2004, will be felt for years. For now, the feeling is one of disbelief, shock, and terrible sorrow. As the 2005 season looms in the foreground, how the team bounces back will be a theme that is closely followed.

Sam Sharpe

RANDY DORTON:
A SHARED LIFE

Watching the final few laps of the last Martinsville race of 2004, I was impressed once again by how smoothly Jimmie Johnson was handling the rest of the field as he had done throughout the year. When the race ended and the victory lane celebrations for Jimmie and his Chad Knaus–led crew were aborted, I couldn't remember ever seeing that before in all my work in the sport since the mid-1980s.

Then, when the network cut to Jim Hunter for an announcement, I'll confess I thought he was going to announce that Bill France Jr. had passed. But when he softly said a Hendrick Motorsports plane had gone down earlier in the day, I was immediately taut. I knew that when races were close to the Charlotte area, many of the Hendrick team and management flew in on race day.

I have to admire Hunter and NASCAR for not releasing the names of the people on that ill-fated plane, even though I suspect he knew then that none had survived, and that the families had not been notified. The local Charlotte TV news channels were not so respectful and restrained, and within a few minutes of Hunter's somber announcement, they were saying that John Hendrick, Ricky Hendrick, and Randy Dorton of Hendrick Motorsports were killed in the crash. I felt a ball of grief move up my chest.

Randy Dorton had been a friend and supporter of *Circle Track* magazine, and later *Stock Car Racing*, since early 1992, when I was the new editor of *Circle Track* and moved to North Carolina to establish our current office at Lowe's (then Charlotte) Motor Speedway. The Hendrick Motorsports complex is only a couple of miles from our editorial offices at Lowe's, and since I had worked on racing ignitions with Randy and the Hendrick engine builders when employed at MSD Ignition, it was natural for me to follow up. It was the beginning of a productive and mutual relationship and friendship.

What an invaluable and trusted resource Randy was for our magazines and for me. There was never an engine technical question I had, whether it be on NASCAR or F1 or late-model or jet-ski engines, that he would not take the time to answer. He might call me back late at night a few days after my initial query, but he never failed to answer. I like to think I have a somewhat technical grasp of race engines, but Randy would take me to the edge of my knowledge, then patiently educate and enlighten me when my mind ran out of talent and awareness. He worked on the cutting edge of the internal combustion engine and never stopped learning about it or sharing his knowledge (to a point, understandably).

Other times, when I wanted to get a read on a particular NASCAR action or line of thinking, he'd give me his unvarnished view for background, and would refer me to a valuable contact for more information. Because he trusted our relationship and our publishing ethics, he gave us access to information at Hendrick Motorsports that helped raise our technical and professional standard. All I can say is that I'm grateful he chose to do so, and my professional and personal values are the better for it.

Not that Randy wasn't above a little partisanship once in a while. He'd sometimes suggest article ideas, particularly ones about proposed NASCAR engine or aero rule changes that might counter GM's momentum, and supply ample technical reasoning on why these changes were not in the best interest of racing overall. But no matter the nature of our contact, I always felt that our magazines and I, and ultimately our readers, were getting the better end of the deal, that we came out of it with an increased knowledge of the sport we cared about because of this man's generosity of spirit.

I can't help but think he learned some of that generosity from his older brother Keith Dorton, who still contributes his time and knowledge and excellence to our titles. Randy

started on his illustrious career when he began working at Keith's engine shop. I can say without equivocation that Randy may not have learned everything he knew about engines from Keith, but he learned something about honest work, how to treat people, and how to strive for excellence from his older brother. Randy chose to incorporate and share those core attributes with many in his life, and we were privileged to know him, and worked at our best because of him. He will be missed.

— Glen Grissom

Randy Dorton *SCR Archives*

Born: August 4, 1971
Hometown: Vallejo, California
Height: 5-7
Weight: 150 pounds
Sponsor: DuPont
Make: Chevrolet
Crew Chief: Robbie Loomis
Owner: Rick Hendrick

Driver Highlights

69 career victories
Four-time Winston Cup champion (1995, 1997, 1998, 2001)
Two-time Daytona 500 winner (1997, 1999)
Four-time Brickyard 400 winner (1994, 1998, 2001, 2004)

Five-time Southern 500 winner (1995, 1996, 1997, 1998, 2002)
1997 Winston Million winner
Four-time Winston No Bull 5 winner
Three-time champion of The Winston (1995, 1997, 2001)
Holds a record seven road course victories

2004: Finished third in points
2003: Finished fourth in points and won at Martinsville twice
2002: Finished fourth in points
2001: NASCAR champion
1999: Daytona 500 winner
1998: NASCAR champion
1997: NASCAR champion
1997: NASCAR 500 winner
1995: NASCAR champion

Busch Series Career Totals

Starts	Championships	Wins	Top 5	Top 10	Avg. Start	Avg. Finish	Winnings
73	0	5	21	32	11.6	13.7	$736,376

Year	Rank	Points	Starts	Wins	Top 5	Top 10	Avg. Start	Avg. Finish	Winning
2000	57	637	5	1	2	3	19.0	14.3	$132,125
1999	51	878	6	1	4	4	5.1	9.1	$139,150
1992	4	4053	31	3	10	15	8.4	12.2	$367,57
1991	11	3582	30	0	5	10	15.3	15.3	$97,123
1990	115	0	1	0	0	0	2.0	39.0	$400

Winston/Nextel Cup Series Career Totals

Year	Races	Wins	Top 5s	Top 10s	Poles	Total Points	Final Standing	Winnings
1992	1	0	0	0	0	70	—	$6,285
1993	30	0	7	11	1	3,447	14th	$765,168
1994	31	2	7	14	1	3,776	8th	$1,779,523
1995	31	7	17	23	8	4,614	1st	$4,347,343
1996	31	10	21	24	5	4,620	2nd	$3,428,485
1997	32	10	22	23	1	4,710	1st	$6,375,658
1998	33	13	26	28	7	5,328	1st	$9,306,584
1999	34	7	18	21	7	4,620	6th	$5,858,633
2000	34	3	11	22	3	4,361	9th	$3,001,144
2001	36	6	18	24	6	5,112	1st	$10,879,757
2002	36	3	13	20	3	4,607	4th	$4,981,170
2003	36	3	15	20	4	4,785	4th	$5,107,762
2004	36	5	16	25	6	6,490	3rd	$6,437,660

INDEX

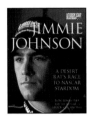

Jimmie Johnson
ISBN: 0-7603-2020-9

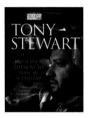

Tony Stewart
ISBN: 0-7603-1855-7

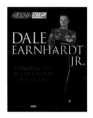

Dale Earnhardt Jr.
ISBN: 0-7603-1517-5

NASCAR's Next Generation
ISBN: 0-7603-1518-3

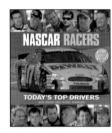

**NASCAR Racers:
Today's Top Drivers**
ISBN: 0-7603-1981-2

Jeff Gordon
ISBN: 0-7603-0952-3

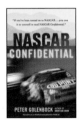

NASCAR Confidential
ISBN: 0-7603-1483-7

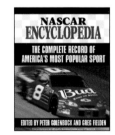

NASCAR Encyclopedia
ISBN: 0-7603-1571-X

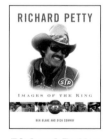

**Richard Petty:
Images of the King**
ISBN: 0-7603-2041-1